Uneasy Neighbors

Uneasy Neighbors

Israel and the European Union

Sharon Pardo and Joel Peters

LEXINGTON BOOKS
A DIVISION OF
ROWMAN & LITTLEFIELD PUBLISHERS, INC.
Lanham • Boulder • New York • Toronto • Plymouth, UK

Published by Lexington Books
A division of Rowman & Littlefield Publishers, Inc.
A wholly owned subsidiary of The Rowman & Littlefield Publishing Group, Inc.
4501 Forbes Boulevard, Suite 200, Lanham, Maryland 20706
http://www.lexingtonbooks.com

Estover Road, Plymouth PL6 7PY, United Kingdom

British Library Cataloguing in Publication Information Available

Library of Congress Cataloging-in-Publication Data
Pardo, Sharon, 1971–
  Uneasy neighbors : Israel and the European Union / Sharon Pardo and Joel Peters.
     p. cm.
  Includes bibliographical references and index.
  ISBN 978-0-7391-2755-1 (cloth : alk. paper) — ISBN 978-0-7391-2756-8 (pbk : alk.
paper) — ISBN 978-0-7391-4470-1 (electronic)
  1. European Union—Israel. 2. Israel—Foreign relations—European Union countries.
3. European Union countries—Foreign relations—Israel. I. Peters, Joel. II. Title.
  DS119.8.E9P37 2010
  327.569404—dc22   2009038880

♾ ™ The paper used in this publication meets the minimum requirements of
American National Standard for Information Sciences—Permanence of Paper
for Printed Library Materials, ANSI/NISO Z39.48-1992.

Printed in the United States of America

~

Contents

Tables and Figures

Tables

Figures

~

Abbreviations

AA	The 1995 EU-Israel Association Agreement
ACRS	Arms Control and Regional Security
AMA	Israeli-Palestinian Agreement on Movement and Access
AP	Action Plan
BP	Barcelona Process
CBM	Confidence Building Measures
CEEC	Central and Eastern European Countries
CFSP	Common Foreign and Security Policy
CIP	Competitiveness and Innovation Framework Program
CSBM	Confidence and Security Building Measures
CSCE	Commission on Security and Co-operation in Europe
EAD	Euro-Arab Dialogue
EC	European Community
ECJ	European Court of Justice
ECU	European Currency Unit
EEA	European Economic Area
EEC	European Economic Community
EFTA	European Free Trade Area
EIP	Euro-Israeli Partnership
EMP	Euro-Mediterranean Partnership
ENP	European Neighborhood Policy
EP	European Parliament
EPC	European Political Cooperation

ESDP	European Security and Defense Policy
EU	European Union
EUBAM Rafah	European Union Border Assistance Mission in Rafah
EUPOL-COPPS	European Union Police Mission for the Palestinian Territories
EUSR	European Union Special Representative
FP	Framework Program for Research and Technological Development
FRA	EU's Agency for Fundamental Rights
GNP	Gross National Product
HR	High Representative
ICJ	International Court of Justice
ICT	Information Communication Technology
IDF	Israel Defense Forces
KAS	Konrad-Adenauer-Stiftung
MEMTTA	Middle East and Mediterranean Travel and Tourism Association
MENA	Middle East and North Africa
MENAFIO	Middle East and North Africa Financial Intermediation Organization
MEP	Member of European Parliament
MEPP	Middle East Peace Process
MS	Member State
NGO	Non-Governmental Organization
NMP	Materials and New Production Technologies
OSCE	Organization for Security and Co-operation in Europe
PA	Palestinian Authority
PEGASE	Mécanisme Palestino-Européen de Gestion de l'Aide Socio-Economique
PLC	Palestinian Legislative Council
PLO	Palestine Liberation Organization
REDWG	Regional Economic Development Working Group
SG	Secretary General
SME	Small and Medium-Sized Enterprises
TIM	Temporary International Mechanism
UfM	Union for the Mediterranean
UK	United Kingdom
UN	United Nations
UNIFIL	United Nations Interim Force in Lebanon
US	United States
WMD	Weapons of Mass Destruction

~

Acknowledgments

This book is the outcome of some twenty years of research and numerous conversations on Israeli-European relations. Many of those conversations have taken place at the Centre for the Study of European Politics and Society (CSEPS) at Ben-Gurion University of the Negev (BGU), Israel. Peters was the founding director of the center; Pardo serves as its current director. We would like to thank all our colleagues at BGU and at CSEPS for their continuous support of our work, and especially to David Newman for his friendship and academic leadership. Michal Eskenazi provided invaluable research assistance. Her contribution to this book stretches far beyond simply gathering information. Natasha Khianey (at Virginia Tech) added important support during the latter stages of the book.

Our ideas have benefitted from several conferences and workshops on Israeli-European relations that we have co-organized in recent years with the Konrad-Adenauer-Stiftung (KAS). We are especially grateful to the director of the KAS Israeli office, Lars Hänsel, for his support of those meetings and of the work of CSEPS. We have also gained from the numerous conferences and workshops in Israel and Europe in which we have participated over the past years. We wish to thank all the participants at those meetings for their feedback. Chapter 4 of this book is based on a study conducted under the Network of Excellence *Global Governance, Regionalisation and Regulation: The Role of the EU—GARNET*. An earlier version was published in Sonia Lucarelli and Lorenzo Fioramonti, eds., *External Perception of the European Union as a Global Actor* (Oxon and New York: Routledge, 2009). We are grateful to

Sonia and Lorenzo for their constructive suggestions and comments on the chapter. Chapter 5 draws on a study conducted under the EuroMeSCo Network; an earlier version of the chapter was published as a *EuroMeSCo Paper*, and we are grateful for the input given by Tobias Schumacher.

Finally, we would like to thank all our friends, colleagues, and the numerous Israeli and European officials for the countless conversations, and for sharing their time, ideas and knowledge of Israeli-European relations so freely. Collectively, they have helped shape our ideas and have corrected our errors. As always, any faults and mistakes that remain are ours alone.

Pardo would like to dedicate this book to my parents, Yosef and Hava, who fled Europe to Israel seeking peace, and to Yonatan. Peters would like to dedicate this book to Ari and to Sandra for the joy they bring to my life.

The Centre for the Study of European Politics and Society at Ben-Gurion University of the Negev was established in 2002 with the aim, in part, of providing a greater understanding of the dynamics of Israeli-European relations. It is our hope that this book will contribute to that ongoing effort.

INTRODUCTION

~

Uneasy Neighbors

"Israel is from Europe, but not in Europe."

—Dan Diner, 2007

Reflections on Israeli-European Relations

Israel was one of the first countries to engage in a dialogue with the European Economic Community (EEC), even before the Treaty of Rome establishing the European Community (EC) entered into force. In April 1958 it became the third country, after Greece and the United States (U.S.), to establish a diplomatic mission in Brussels, the "capital" of the newly established European Communities. In February 1959, Israel and the EC formally established full diplomatic relations.

Yet, despite this early interest, for many years Europe did not figure highly in Israeli foreign policy. Several reasons can be forwarded: historical factors such as the Jewish experience in Europe and the Holocaust; the positions adopted by European states on the Arab-Israeli conflict (individually and collectively) after the Six Day War in 1967 and beyond; the centrality of the United States in Israeli diplomatic and strategic thinking; and the European Union's (EU) inability to develop an effective common foreign policy toward Israel. These factors, among others, have pushed Israel to behave more as an island in the middle of the Atlantic Ocean than a Mediterranean country neighboring the European continent.

Over the years, however, Israel and Europe have gradually drawn closer together, creating an ever-increasing network of economic, scientific and cultural ties. Those relations have consisted of a number of conflicting trends leading to the emergence of a troubled and, at times, volatile relationship. A thriving economic partnership, yet a relationship, at the political level, that has been marked by disappointment, bitterness and anger. Today, the EU is Israel's most important trading partner. The EU is Israel's largest source of imports and is its second-largest export market. In 2008 Israel was ranked as the EU's twenty-fifth-largest trading partner, with total trade between the two economies amounting to approximately €25.3 billion.[1] For Israel, that meant that 34 percent of its imports (excluding diamonds) came from the EU, and 33 percent of its exports (excluding diamonds) were directed to the European market.[2] Politically, Israel has displayed a genuine desire to strengthen its ties with Europe and to be included as part of the European project. On the other hand, Israelis are deeply suspicious of European policies, and are untrusting of Europe's intentions toward the Arab-Israeli conflict and to the region as a whole. European leaders have displayed an equally ambivalent attitude concerning the nature of its ties with Israel. For its part, European leaders talk of their desire to develop a "special relationship" with Israel. Yet they have failed to articulate what such a status might actually entail.

Notwithstanding the importance and relevance of Israeli-European relations, this subject has received relatively little attention in the fields of Israeli, European and Middle East studies, outside the context of the Arab-Israeli conflict. A review of the literature reveals a limited number of studies on Israeli-EU relations. This book aims to fill this gap. It offers an analysis of the dynamics of Israeli-European relations and discusses significant developments in that relationship from the late 1950s through to the present day. The book does not set out to address all aspects of Israeli-European relations, nor does it cover the specific nature of the varied and extensive set of bilateral relations between Israel and the individual member states of the EU. Rather, the emphasis is placed on five broad themes that address different dimensions of the relationship between Israel and the EU. Although the chapters are designed to add up to an inclusive study of Israeli-European relations, they can also be read as separate, stand-alone, essays.

The opening chapter covers the issue that has dominated Israeli-European relations for the past three decades—the Israeli-Palestinian conflict. Over the years EU member states have been angered by their marginalization in the efforts to resolve the conflict and have sought to play a greater role in the Middle East peace process commensurate with the EU's global standing.

The chapter focuses on Israeli policies toward the conflict and on European positions and responses to those policies. It discusses how the differences over the resolution of the Israeli-Palestinian conflict have impacted on the development and the nature of Israeli-European relations.

At the same time, Israel and the EU have over the past twenty years been engaged in a series of multilateral regional frameworks in which the EU has been directly responsible for the management of relations between Israel and the Arab world. The second chapter explores these multilateral initiatives and evaluates the role the EU has played in three of them: the Multilateral Arab-Israeli Talks, the Euro-Mediterranean Partnership (the Barcelona Process), and the Union for the Mediterranean. Europe's inability to mediate Israeli-Arab tensions within these multilateral frameworks has impacted negatively on perceptions of the EU within Israel and the development of Israeli-European relations. The chapter argues that without significant progress being made on resolving the Israeli-Palestinian conflict a true regional cooperative security structure is extremely unlikely, if not impossible, and that Israeli-European relations need to be developed outside the context of these multilateral frameworks.

Given the failings of these multilateral structures, the pivot of Israel's relations with the EU remains a bilateral one. The third chapter surveys the evolution and dynamics of this bilateral relationship. As their economic and political interests have become increasingly intertwined, Israel and the EU have sought to create an institutional framework to facilitate commercial ties, scientific cooperation and foster a political dialogue. The chapter discusses in detail the 1995 Association Agreement and the 2004 EU-Israel Action Plan. The chapter concludes with a discussion of recent efforts toward upgrading Israel's formal standing with the EU.

The fourth chapter explores the changing images and perceptions in Israel of the EU among the general public and political elites, organized civil society and the Israeli press. An evaluation of the perceptions held by Israelis allows for a better understanding of the challenges Israel and the EU have to overcome in order to put Israeli-European relations on a more stable footing. The chapter reveals that Israelis hold contradictory views about relations with the EU. On the one hand, Israelis feel that the EU represents a hospitable framework for Israeli accession, and as a result Israel should explore joining the EU in the near future. Yet at the same time, they believe strongly that anti-Israeli attitudes are deeply embedded within the EU, and that its geo-political and geo-strategic views are detrimental to the security of Israel.

The fifth chapter turns to the future of Israeli-European relations. Israeli and European leaders have talked in recent years about upgrading Israel's formal standing with the EU. Little thought has been given to the institutional arrangements that would govern this "upgraded" status. This chapter meets that challenge. We present a new model, the "Euro-Israeli Partnership" (EIP), which offers an institutional structure below the level of full EU membership.

The book concludes by addressing the underlying tensions and grievances that have accounted for the difficulties in the Israeli-European relationship. It argues that Israelis and Europeans need to discuss not only what unites them but also what divides them. This dialogue needs to be based on an open, honest and frank exchange of ideas, aimed at developing a deeper understanding of their differences and of their divergent values. By developing such a dialogue over current issues, future tensions, most notably over the Arab-Israeli conflict, can be better mediated. The chapter evaluates not only the shortcomings but also the achievements of this relationship and provides a set of ideas about the future direction of Israeli-European relations. A study of Israeli-European relations is of value beyond the exploration of the dynamics of this unusual relationship. An analysis of European policies toward Israel offers an interesting case study of the Union's emerging role as an international actor, especially in the Middle East.

A Note on Terminology and Sources

Since the book spans the history of fifty years of Israeli-European relations, it is necessary to clarify our use of several terms. The terms "Israeli-European relations" and "Israeli-EC/EU relations" are used interchangeably to refer to ties between Israel and the EU since 1957. We prefer the term "Europe" as a generic term for the EU, its institutions and member states. Under the 1992 Treaty on European Union (the Maastricht Treaty) the European Community (EC) was included under the new structure of the EU. For brevity, throughout the book, we generally refer to the EU despite legal distinctions between the EC and the EU.

Many aspects of Israeli-European relations remain classified and as such many documents, reports and diplomatic exchanges are not available to researchers and the general public. Our analysis is based on published sources and documents. We have supplemented this information with numerous interviews with Israeli and European politicians, policy makers, officials, journalists and representatives of non-governmental organizations (NGOs).

—Sharon Pardo and Joel Peters
August 2009

CHAPTER ONE

∿

Israel, Europe and the Israeli-Palestinian Peace Process
From Divergence to Convergence

"The European Union is determined to develop a close partnership with Israel. The process of developing a closer EU-Israel partnership needs to be, and to be seen, in the context of the broad range of our common interests and objectives which notably include the resolution of the Israeli-Palestinian conflict through the implementation of the two-state solution."

—Statement of the European Union, 2008

At the eighth meeting of the EU-Israel Association Council in June 2008, the EU responded positively to Israel's request to upgrade its relations with the Union.[1] In December 2008 at the Brussels Council of Ministers meeting, the EU presented a series of concrete proposals to achieve this goal.[2] Within weeks of the Brussels meeting, Israel launched Operation Cast Lead in response to the breakdown of the cease-fire between Israel and Hamas and the launching of missiles attacks from Gaza on Israeli cities in the south of the country. European leaders were outspoken in their criticism of Israel's 22-day military (re)invasion of Gaza, which left more than 1,400 Palestinians dead, and of Israel's subsequent economic blockade of Gaza. Tensions between Israel and the EU were further exacerbated over the refusal of the new Likud-led government to support the creation of a Palestinian state. By the time of the ninth meeting of the EU-Israel Association Council in June 2009, all talk of an upgrade by the EU of its relations with Israel had been dropped.

Without question, it is the friction over the Israeli-Palestinian conflict that has most soured Israeli-European relations for the past three decades. European states have been angered by their marginalization over the years in the efforts to resolve the conflict and believe Europe should be afforded a role in the peace process commensurate with its global standing. Israeli policies toward the conflict and European responses to those policies have had a critical impact on the development of bilateral relations, and the ways in which Israeli and European societies have viewed each other.

From Venice to Oslo

The desire of EU member states to carve out a distinct and common stance toward the Middle East, independent of the superpowers, and to promote a collective role in bringing about a peaceful resolution to the Israeli-Palestinian conflict can be traced back to the early 1970s. Efforts to draw up a common set of principles to guide their policies toward the conflict were a central feature of the initial years of European Political Cooperation (EPC). Given Europe's historical legacy, its geographical proximity to the region and its extensive network of political, economic and cultural ties, member states saw the Middle East as a region ripe for EU policy coordination.

The first official declaration on the Arab-Israeli conflict within the framework of EPC was issued on 6 November 1973 in the aftermath of the Yom Kippur War. The declaration spoke of the inadmissibility of the acquisition of territories by force and called on Israel to end its occupation of Arab land. It also determined that in order to secure a just and lasting peace to the conflict the *legitimate rights* of the Palestinians needed to be taken into account. The declaration also made reference to two sensitive issues which Israel had long rejected: that Arab-Israeli negotiations should take place within the framework of the UN; and that any peace agreement should be secured by "international guarantees." Subsequent declarations and joint texts issued by the EC in the 1970s referred not just to the "legitimate rights" of the Palestinians but also of their right "to express a national identity," a phrase that was to become standard in all European texts on the Arab-Israeli conflict. At the June 1977 London European Council meeting the Nine (EC member states) sharpened their position further, now calling for the inclusion of representatives of the Palestinian people in any future negotiations to resolve the conflict, and, in language reminiscent of the "Balfour declaration," that a just and lasting solution demanded "a homeland for the Palestinian people."

The Yom Kippur War also led to the launching of the Euro-Arab Dialogue (EAD) as a response to the oil crisis triggered by the war. This dialogue was intended by the Europeans to be a forum aimed at addressing future economic and technical cooperation between Europe and the Arab world. But it quickly became politicized by the Arab states, who sought to transform it into an arena for addressing the Palestinian question. In statements emanating from the EAD, European states called for a halt to the construction of Israeli settlements in the occupied territories and expressed their opposition to unilateral initiatives that would change the status of Jerusalem.[3]

Unsurprisingly, these statements together with the creation of the EAD were dismissed by Israel as indicative of European appeasement and of its pandering to the Arab world in light of its newfound oil-power and wealth. The Israeli reaction to the 6 November 1973 declaration was sharp and set the tone for subsequent Israeli responses to European initiatives and statements on the conflict. For Israel, the EC was motivated by the need to persuade the Arab states not to reduce the supply of oil. Israeli foreign minister Abba Eban dismissed the declaration as "oil for Europe" not "peace in the Middle East" and bluntly informed the Europeans that if they wanted to contribute to a negotiated settlement they should refrain from issuing such declarations in the future.[4]

The EC responded unenthusiastically to the signing of the Camp David Accords between Israel and Egypt in September 1978 and the subsequent Egyptian-Israeli Peace Treaty of March 1979. The EC qualified its support for the Camp David Accords by reiterating its view that a lasting and just peace in the Middle East could only take place within the context of a comprehensive settlement that would provide Palestinians with a homeland. When the Camp David Process began to flounder over the issue of Palestinian autonomy, the EC launched its own initiative with the Venice declaration of 13 June 1980.

In issuing the Venice declaration, Europe gave notice of its aspirations to play a greater role in the Arab-Israeli conflict. In the preamble to the declaration, the members of the EC stated that "[. . .] the traditional ties and common interests which link Europe to the Middle East" obligated them "[. . .] to play a 'special role' in the pursuit of regional peace." The Venice declaration outlined a number of principles which have defined Europe's vision toward the resolution of the Israeli-Palestinian conflict ever since. These principles were not a radical departure in European thinking. Rather, they crystallized positions that had evolved gradually over the previous decade. The declaration asserted that it was imperative that a just resolution be found to the Palestinian problem, and that this issue should not be viewed as simply a refugee problem. In the eyes of the Nine, a just and lasting solution to the conflict demanded that "the Palestinian people be allowed to exercise fully its rights to self-determination."

In addition to spelling out what was required for a viable solution to the Arab-Israeli conflict, the Europeans castigated Israel for its settlement policy: "[The EC] is deeply convinced that the Israeli settlements constitute a serious obstacle to the peace process in the Middle East. The Nine consider that these settlements, as well as modifications in population and property in the occupied Arab territories, are illegal under international law." They also warned Israel over its policy in Jerusalem: "The Nine stress that they will not accept any unilateral initiative designed to change the status of Jerusalem." The Venice declaration also outlined the diplomatic steps needed to be taken in order to achieve a lasting resolution of the Palestinian question. Specifically, and to the anger of Israel, it called for the inclusion of the Palestine Liberation Organization (PLO) in any future negotiating process aimed at resolving the conflict.[5]

Israel's response was furious and uncompromising. For Israel, European states were ready to sacrifice Israel's safety in order to protect its oil supplies and commercial dealings with the Arab world. In a statement evoking memories of Europe's past and of World War II, Israel denounced the European position:

> Nothing will remain of the Venice Resolution but its bitter memory. The Resolution calls upon us, and other nations, to include in the peace process the Arab S.S. known as "The Palestine Liberation Organization." . . . For a "peace," which would be achieved with the participation of that same organization of murderers, a number of European countries are willing to give guarantees, even military ones. Anyone with a memory will shudder at this, knowing the consequences of the guarantee given to Czechoslovakia in 1938, after the Sudetenland was torn from it, also for the sake of self-determination. Israel does not seek a guarantee for its security from any European nation. . . . Any man of good will and any free person in Europe who would examine this document would see in it a Munich-like surrender, the second in our generation, to tyranic extortion, and an encouragement to all the elements which aspire to defeat the peace process in the Middle East.[6]

From the perspective of today, the Venice declaration looks less radical and threatening to Israeli security. Most of the principles outlined reflect the basis of the current round of Israeli-Palestinian negotiations. However, the issuing of the declaration in June 1980 marked a turning point in Israeli-

European relations adding a charged political undertone to what had previously been a primarily economic relationship. Almost thirty years on, it remains a defining moment in Israeli discourse and in the public distrust of Europe as a potential mediator in the Arab-Israeli peace process. The Venice declaration signaled a low point in Israel's relations with the EU from which they have never fully recovered.

Venice cast a large shadow over Israeli-European relations throughout the 1980s. From the issuing of the declaration in June 1980 to the convening of the Madrid peace conference in November 1991, Israel vigorously opposed any European attempt to play a significant role in the peace process. Israel was especially angered by the stream of European declarations on the conflict following Israel's invasion of Lebanon in 1982 and the outbreak of the first Palestinian *intifada* in December 1987. Those European statements became increasingly critical of Israeli policies and more forthright in their endorsement of the PLO and the right of the Palestinians to national self-determination. The outbreak of the *intifada* triggered harsh criticism of Israel across Europe for its forceful response to the Palestinian uprising and drew widespread sympathy for the Palestinian cause in European capitals. In response, Israelis were united in their criticism of Europe's approach to the conflict, which they saw as expressing little concern for Israel's well-being and security and as simply mirroring the Arab point of view. They denounced Europe's approach to the conflict for its impartiality and for the way it was making increasing demands on Israel to make concessions without making similar calls on the Arab side for reciprocal measures.

European diplomacy in the 1980s did little to advance its ambitions of playing a more significant role in bringing the Arab-Israeli conflict to a peaceful end. Europe possessed little leverage over Israel, and its voice was studiously ignored in Jerusalem. In January 1989, Israeli prime minister Yitzhak Shamir bluntly informed Lord Plumb, the president of the European Parliament, that Israel did not regard Europe as a partner and saw it as playing no part in the political process in the Middle East on account of its pro-Palestinian bias.

With the end of the first Gulf war in the summer of 1991, the U.S. turned its attention to the Arab-Israeli conflict. Europe expected to play its part in the diplomatic efforts to revive the peace process. These hopes were short-lived. At the insistence of Israel, the EU was excluded from any significant role. While the U.S. turned to Spain to host an international conference to (re)launch the Arab-Israeli peace process, the EC played a marginal role in the proceedings of the Madrid conference of November 1991. Europeans were further incensed that the U.S. turned to Moscow to serve as co-sponsor to the Madrid conference, despite the fact that the Soviet Union's power was visibly receding, and that it was on the point of collapse.

In the end, the framework devised by the U.S. proved to be insufficient to bring about a breakthrough in the negotiations between Israel and the Palestinians. It took a secret back channel, under the gentle guidance of the Norwegians, for Israel and the PLO to put aside their differences and sit down together. European states could draw a sense of satisfaction that a policy that they had been advocating since 1980, namely the need to involve the PLO directly in any negotiations, had finally been adopted by Israel. In reality, however, the Venice declaration and subsequent diplomatic strategies adopted by the EU had little impact on the Arab-Israeli conflict, or in bringing Israel and the PLO together. The EU might have drawn the right conclusions thirteen years previously, but it had failed to translate its declarations and statements on the Middle East into any effective operative strategy. Israel paid little heed to European advice and ideas. Prior to the signing of the Oslo Accords, rightly or wrongly, the EU was regarded by Israel as part of the problem and not part of the solution.

The Oslo Process

The EU played no role in the lead up to the Madrid conference nor in the bilateral negotiations that immediately followed the conference. Instead it was consigned to operating within the framework of the five working groups of the multilateral talks which were set up by the Madrid conference. The EU was entrusted with the running of the Regional Economic Development Working Group (REDWG), the largest of the five working groups and the sphere which best reflected the goal of the multilateral track of promoting regional cooperation. Such was Israel's distrust of Europe's intentions in the region that it invested few diplomatic resources in the initial meetings of the REDWG working group, and it was adamant that no European states be invited to participate in the discussions of the Arms Control and Regional Security (ACRS) working group.

The breakthrough between Israel and the PLO with the signing of the Oslo Accords in September 1993 led to a marked transformation in Israeli-European relations in both tone and substance. Israel began to lavish praise on Europe, seeing it as a model for putting aside past hatreds and for building new cooperative structures for peace and stability. Shimon Peres' vision of a "new Middle East"[7] drew direct parallels with Europe's experience in the aftermath of World War II. European leaders became welcome visitors in Jerusalem. This new atmosphere in Israeli-European relations found expression at the heads of state meeting at Essen in December 1994 with the European leaders declaring: "that Israel on account of its high level of economic development should enjoy special status in its relations with the EU on the basis of reciprocity and common interest."[8] One year later, Israel and the EU put their signatures to a new trade agreement. The EU-Israel Association Agreement (AA) was a significant upgrade of the 1975 cooperation agreement, which had governed economic ties for the previous two decades. The Association Agreement created new provisions for the liberalization of services, new rules for the movement of capital, simplifying trade conditions and the free movement of goods and for the inclusion of Israel as a full member of Europe's research and development program. The Association Agreement also established a framework for an ongoing political dialogue at the ministerial, senior official and parliamentary level, capped by an Association Council that would meet annually.[9]

Israel looked to Europe to become directly engaged in the peace process through the offering of financial support to the Palestinian economy, and by building the institutional capacity of the Palestinians in the West Bank and Gaza. Europe quickly became the mainstay of the international donor effort to the Palestinians. On the eve of the signing of the Declaration of Principles, the EC announced that it would be releasing an immediate aid package of ECU 35 million to enable the PLO to establish services and attend to the most urgent needs of the Palestinians. At the donors conference held on 1 October 1993, the member states of the EU collectively pledged an additional ECU 500 million, spread over a period of five years, for the economic recovery and the developmental needs of the Palestinian territories. This aid package amounted to nearly a quarter of the total funds pledged by the participants at the Washington conference and made the EU the leading donor to the Palestinians. The EU also provided $24 million for logistical preparations and was responsible for the monitoring of elections to the new Palestinian Legislative Council (PLC), held at the beginning of January 1996. To underline their commitment to the long-term development of the Palestinian economy, the European Commission and the PLO initialed on 10 December 1996 a Euro-Mediterranean Interim Association Agreement on Trade and Cooperation for the benefit of the Palestinian Authority.

Through its economic commitment to the Palestinians, Europe acquired a direct and material interest in ensuring that progress was maintained in the peace process. As such they became increasingly critical during the Oslo process of Israeli security policies and the economic restrictions imposed on the West Bank and Gaza. The member states of the EU did not hide their frustration that, on account of Israel's actions, their financial support was required to meet the immediate shortfall in the Palestinian budget and in covering the day-to-day running costs of the Palestinian Authority rather than contributing toward the future welfare and long-term development of the Palestinian economy.

Europe's growing irritation at its marginalization from the political process was most palpable during Binyamin Netanyahu's first tenure as prime minister of Israel when the peace process virtually ground to a halt. For European leaders, Netanyahu's policies were at best unhelpful, and at worst catastrophic. At the beginning of October 1996, the EU expressed its concern at the outbreak of rioting in Gaza and the West Bank, which had erupted following the opening of the Hasmonean Tunnel in the old city of Jerusalem in September, resulting in the deaths of 64 Palestinians and 15 Israeli soldiers. The EU essentially held Israel responsible for the outbreak of violence, which had been "precipitated by frustration and exasperation at the absence of any real progress in the Peace Process and [the EU] firmly believes that the absence of such progress is the root cause of the unrest." EU officials also privately hinted that Israel's actions were placing the ratification of the new trade agreement under risk.

The sense of European frustration was best described by Rosemary Hollis:

> It is no longer possible for Israel, or more to the point the United States, to sideline Europeans in their strategies for the region. Singly and collectively the Europeans have too much at stake in the Middle East to defer to the United States' lead, if, as latterly, it seems unable by itself to rescue the Arab-Israeli peace process from a reversion to confrontation.[10]

Speaking to the Middle East and North Africa Economic Conference held in Cairo, in November 1996, the Irish foreign minister Dick Spring informed the meeting of Europe's determination to play a more active role: "[The EU] had a responsibility both to the region and to itself to put the peace process back on track."

The clearest sign of Europe's intent was the decision in October 1996 to appoint a special envoy to the peace process, a position that was initially filled by Miguel Moratinos, who had previously served as the Spanish ambassador to Israel. The decision to appoint a special envoy to the region was greeted with skepticism by Israel who saw it as yet a further sign of renewed European efforts to meddle in the peace process and to win the affection of the Arabs. The appointment of Moratinos, in preference to the high-profile political appointee originally envisaged by some European states, was, however, quietly welcomed. The assigning of a special envoy offered the EU more visibility in the region but did little to change Israel's views of the value of European mediation. For the better part of the Oslo process, until its collapse at the end of 2000, Moratinos cut a marginal figure. The EU was unable to exact any defined role for itself nor influence events. When Israel and the Palestinians met at Camp David in July 2000 to discuss final status issues it played no part in the proceedings, and watched firmly from the sidelines.

Israeli-European relations nose-dived during Netanyahu's first term as Israel's prime minister, reaching a new low with the issuing of the Berlin declaration in March 1999, in which the EU supported Palestinian state-hood.[11] Israel and Europe repeatedly clashed over Israeli restrictions of the freedom of movement of Palestinians, the expansion of Israeli settlements in the West Bank and Gaza and most notably over differences on the status of Jerusalem.

Israel, the EU and the Future of Jerusalem

Differences over the status and the future of Jerusalem have been a par-ticular source of friction between Israel and Europe. European states never recognized Israel's annexation of East Jerusalem in 1967 and have consis-tently warned Israel from taking unilateral measures which would alter the character of the city. For Europe, the key to resolving the Israeli-Palestinian conflict comprises the establishment of a Palestinian state with Jerusalem as its capital.

Of particular concern to Europeans has been the construction and expan-sion of Jewish neighborhoods in East Jerusalem, the closure of Palestinian institutions in Jerusalem, the restriction of work permits and changes in residency rules for Palestinians, and, since 2002, the construction of Israel's separation barrier/wall/fence around Jerusalem. A report issued by the EU in 2006 saw Israel's actions in Jerusalem as designed deliberately to reduce the possibility of reaching a final status agreement on Jerusalem that any Pales-tinian could possibly accept, and to demonstrate a clear Israeli intention of turning the annexation of East Jerusalem into a concrete fact. The report was also fearful that Israeli measures would "risk radicalising the hitherto relatively quiescent Palestinian population of East Jerusalem."[12]

Israel has been incensed by the tone and the wording of European criti-cism of its policies and actions. European references to Jewish neighborhoods in East Jerusalem as *settlements* and determining their construction as *illegal*, thereby not distinguishing them, in European eyes, from Israeli settlements in the West Bank and Gaza, is seen as a direct challenge to Israel's claim to Jerusalem as its undivided capital. For Israelis, the wording of European statements on Jerusalem mirrors the language used by the Palestinians and is further reflective of European biases toward the Israeli-Palestinian conflict.

The terse exchange between Israel and Europe over the opening of the Hasmonean Tunnel in September 1996 highlights the tension over the status of Jerusalem. The European Council of Ministers immediately called upon Israel to close the tunnel and refrain from taking unilateral steps that might be "likely to create mistrust about its intentions" and to cease "all acts that might affect the Holy Places in Jerusalem." The statement spelled out Europe's position on the legal status of Jerusalem and the non-recognition of Israel's annexation of East Jerusalem:

> East Jerusalem is subject to the principles set out in the UN Security Council Resolution 242, notably the inadmissibility of the acquisition of territory by force and therefore is not under Israeli sovereignty. The Union asserts that the Fourth Geneva Convention is fully applicable to East Jerusalem, as it is to other territories under occupation.

The Israeli government dismissed the European charges in a tone reminiscent of its denunciation of the Venice declaration and other European statements. Efforts for peace in the Middle East would not be helped: "by a partial European position or by language that could have a threatening tone . . . Europe's desire to contribute to the peace process should not be manifested by adopting positions that could hinder the peace process and the negotiations aimed to promote it."[13]

Tensions between Israel and Europe over Jerusalem have not just been confined to rhetorical exchanges. Differences over the status of Jerusalem have resulted in a number of high-profile crises and diplomatic clashes, especially during Binyamin Netanyahu's first tenure as Israel's prime minister. Shortly after the opening of the Hasmonean Tunnel, French president Jacques Chirac toured the Muslim Quarter of the Old City of Jerusalem. Chirac refused to be accompanied by Israeli officials during his visit, a symbolic gesture of France's non-recognition of Israeli sovereignty over the Old City.[14] Two issues in particular, the closure of the Orient House and the construction of Har Homa/Jabal Abu Ghneim, became emblematic of deeper underlying tensions between Israel and Europe.

The Orient House
Until 1996, delegations from the EU made regular high-level visits to Orient House, the office of Faisal Husseini who held the Jerusalem portfolio

on the PLO Executive Committee. For example, in February 1995 the EU Troika foreign ministers met with Palestinian leaders in the Orient House as part of their visit to the region, as did EU Council president Javier Solana later on in the year. The Israeli government was highly critical of these and other visits, seeing them as a diplomatic challenge by European leaders to Israel's claim of sovereignty over East Jerusalem, and as lending support to Palestinian claims in Jerusalem by bestowing on Orient House the status of a quasi-foreign ministry.

Israel sought to block these visits and frequently threatened to close down the Orient House. It charged that by receiving foreign representatives at the Orient House the Palestinians were in breach of agreements within the Oslo Accords, which prohibited political activities of the Palestinian Authority in Jerusalem. Israel's refusal to allow the EU Troika, led by the Irish foreign minister, to visit Orient House in November 1996 led to the EU canceling the Troika's visit to Israel, a move dismissed by the Israeli foreign ministry as "not such a catastrophe."[15] Under the immediate threat to close down the Orient House by the Netanyahu government, the EU eventually agreed to stop official visits. This decision eased tensions with Israel over this issue but only at the margins. Diplomatic and political representatives from individual EU member states continued to visit Orient House and EU officials held meetings with Palestinian leaders in the vicinity of Orient House or in locations elsewhere in East Jerusalem. In March 1999, Israel's foreign minister wrote to the EU protesting these meetings and demanding that they stop. The German ambassador to Israel responded sternly on behalf of the EU, reminding Israel that the EU did not recognize Israeli sovereignty over East Jerusalem and that EU representatives would continue their practice of meeting with Palestinian representatives.

Israel eventually closed the Orient House in April 2001, following a series of terrorist attacks in Jerusalem, to the protest of the EU. The Orient House remains a charged issue. In a strategy paper on the peace process, written in November 2008 but not released at that time at the request of Israel, the EU pointed to the importance of reopening of Palestinian institutions in East Jerusalem, specifically mentioning the Orient House and of Europe's intention of working actively toward that aim.[16]

Har Homa/Jabal Abu Ghneim

In March 1997, shortly after the signing of the Hebron redeployment agreement, Israel announced that it intended to start construction of a new Jewish neighborhood at Har Homa, (known as Jabal Abu Ghneim to the Palestinians), a hilltop just north of Bethlehem that Israel had annexed to Jerusalem

in 1967. The decision of the Israeli government led to an international out-
cry. The move was decried for its timing (undercutting the tentative progress
in the peace process) and as a step that would complete the encirclement
of Jerusalem by Jewish neighborhoods, thereby restricting the movement of
Palestinians between Bethlehem and Ramallah. The EU joined the calls for
Israel to reverse its decision, repeating its position that the construction of
settlements anywhere in the occupied territories, including in East Jerusalem,
was illegal under international law.

The following year, the British foreign secretary Robin Cook, in his capacity as the president of the EU Council, announced his intention to visit the
disputed site and to meet with Palestinian representatives as part of his visit
to the region. Israel reacted angrily to Cook's planned visit, seeing it as a provocative move and a further challenge by the EU to its claim of sovereignty
over all of Jerusalem and as a further European attempt to precondition final
status talk on Jerusalem's future. In spite of Israel's objections, Cook traveled
to Har Homa/Jabal Abu Ghneim as planned. Adding insult to injury, Cook's
trip to Jerusalem included laying a wreath commemorating the fiftieth an-
niversary of the Deir Yassin massacre,[17] but did not take in the customary
visit to Yad Vashem, Israel's memorial to the victims of the Holocaust. Israel
saw Cook's visit as deliberately provocative. Israel's prime minister Binyamin
Netanyahu was so enraged by Cook's visit to Har Homa/Jabal Abu Ghneim
that he snubbed him during his visit and canceled a scheduled dinner at the
last minute.

European protests failed to prevent the building of the Har Homa neighborhood, which has now grown to a Jewish residential area of 4,000 families.
But Har Homa/Jabal Abu Ghneim has remained in the spotlight as a symbol
for Europeans of Israel's bad faith and its intentions over the future of Jerusalem. When in 2007 Israel announced a new tender for the construction of
307 additional homes shortly after the Annapolis summit meeting, the EU
joined other international voices in condemning Israel for undermining the
credibility of the newly (re)launched peace process.

Palestinian Statehood

Israel and Europe have been at odds over the years over European support for
Palestinian statehood. European statements in the 1970s and 1980s did not
make any explicit reference for the creation of a Palestinian state. Instead,
they talked of the necessity for *"a homeland for the Palestinian people"* and the
legitimate right of the Palestinian people *"to express a national identity"* and

"to self-determination." Similarly, the Oslo Accords made no direct reference to a Palestinian state. European leaders and a vast majority of European civil society clearly believed, however, that the establishment of a Palestinian state was both a necessary, desired, and inevitable outcome of the peace process.

Throughout the Oslo years, the EU sharpened its formal position on this issue, moving slowly toward an explicit call for Palestinian statehood. In the summer of 1998, in a statement issued by the Council of Ministers following the Cardiff summit meeting, the EU called on "[. . .] Israel to recognise the right of the Palestinians to exercise self-determination, *without excluding the option of a State.*"[18] One year later at the Council of Ministers meeting held in Berlin on 24–25 March 1999, the EU went one step further with its most explicit statement in support of Palestinian statehood by reaffirming "the unqualified Palestinian right to self-determination in the option of a state and looks forward to the early fulfillment of that right." It explained its position:

> The European Union is convinced that the creation of a democratic viable and peaceful sovereign Palestinian state on the basis of existing agreements and through negotiations would be the best guarantee of Israel's security and Israel's acceptance as an equal partner in the region. The European Union declares its readiness to consider the recognition of a Palestinian state in due course. . . .[19]

The wording of the Berlin declaration and the decision to issue such an explicit call for Palestinian statehood was crafted in close coordination with the American government and formed an integral element of the diplomatic efforts aimed at persuading the PLO from making a unilateral declaration of independence on 4 May 1999. Highlighting European support for Palestinian statehood turned out to be an invaluable way of assuring the Palestinians of international support for their claim to statehood, and in preventing them from embarking on such a course, unilaterally and prematurely. Israel did not see it that way. Ignoring the quiet American role behind the declaration, it dismissed the Berlin declaration as an attempt by Europe to determine the future outcomes of the negotiations with the Palestinians. Binyamin Netanyahu's response to the Berlin declaration was unambiguous: "It is a shame that Europe, where a third of the Jewish people were killed, should take a stand which puts Israel at risk and goes against our interest."[20]

It was not until after the collapse of the peace process that the EU called directly for the establishment of a Palestinian state. Endorsing calls for the convening of an international conference to bring Israel and the Palestinians back to the negotiating table, the Seville Council of Ministers meeting in June 2002 detailed the Union's position on the conflict:

> The objective is an end to the occupation and the early establishment of a democratic, viable, peaceful and sovereign State of Palestine, on the basis of the 1967 borders, if necessary with minor adjustments agreed by the parties. The end result should be two States living side by side within secure and recognised borders enjoying normal relations with their neighbours.[21]

For Europe, the creation of a Palestinian state would not only meet the legitimate rights of the Palestinians to self-determination but it was also regarded as the best guarantee for Israel's long-term security.

Israel, the EU and the Separation Wall/Fence

The EU's stress on the need of returning to the negotiating table was out of step, however, with an Israeli public which had lost faith with Yasser Arafat, and in the possibility of peace with the Palestinians. Israel was less interested in resuming negotiations than in developing strategies of containment and separation.

In the summer of 2002, as a result of the continuing violence between Israel and the Palestinians, the Israeli government began the construction of the security barrier, with the aim of creating a physical separation of Israel from the West Bank. Israel's construction of the security barrier, consisting of a concrete wall in the Jerusalem area and in other areas of parallel rows of barbed wire, has been a source of great controversy. Israel has defended the separation fence arguing that its construction is a legitimate act of self-defense in the face of Palestinian terrorism and the continuous suicide bombings launched by Palestinians during the al-Aqsa *intifada*. It has pointed to the separation barrier as the major contributory factor behind the significantly reduced number of incidents of suicide bombings from 2002 to 2009. Critics, on the other hand, have argued that the separation fence is a land-grab, an attempt by Israel to annex Palestinian land under the guise of security, and that it has led to personal and economic sufferings to Palestinians living nearby. Above all, it has the intent or the effect of pre-empting final status negotiations.

From the outset, European states were outspoken in their criticism of Israel, questioning Israel's true motives by referring to the barrier as "Israel's so-called security fence." They were equally critical of the confiscation of Palestinian land for its construction, and expressed their concern over the economic hardships caused to Palestinians as a consequence. At the end of 2003, the UN General Assembly asked the International Court of Justice (ICJ) to give an Advisory Opinion on the legality of the separation barrier. On 9 July 2004, the ICJ ruled that the barrier was a violation of international humanitarian law and human rights law.[22] The fact that all the European judges to the court supported this Advisory Opinion (while the American judge was the only dissenting opinion) was not lost on the Israeli media. Eleven days later, the UN General Assembly voted 150–6 condemning Israel and demanding the immediate dismantlement of the barrier. All 25 member states of the EU, in spite of intensive lobbying by Israel, supported the motion. In response to the European vote the Israeli foreign ministry launched a withering attack: "Israel is particularly disappointed by the European stand. The willingness of the EU to fall in with the Palestinian position, together with its desire to reach a European consensus at the price of descending to the lowest common denominator, raises doubts as to the ability of the EU to contribute anything constructive to the diplomatic process."[23]

Israel's foreign minister Silvan Shalom informed Javier Solana, the EU's high representative for Common Foreign and Security Policy (CFSP), who was visiting Jerusalem two days after the vote in the General Assembly, that the government and people of Israel were deeply disappointed by Europe's decision to join forces with the Palestinians in their opposition to the separation fence. In a joint press conference Shalom rebuked the Europeans for their stance: "The EU should focus its efforts in promoting Palestinian reform," Shalom told Solana, "and not support Palestinian manipulation in the United Nations," adding that Europe's vote only encourages the Palestinians to relinquish their responsibility in fighting terror. In response, Solana was dismissive of Israel's reproach arguing that Europe's vote should not be seen as aimed against Israel. "A country has the right to build a fence on its own territory but we [the EU] believe that the route of this fence is contrary of international law."[24] Solana wrapped up a stormy two-day visit by reminding Israel that the EU held long-standing strategic interests in the region and bluntly informing his hosts that Europe intended to play a role in the peace process whether Israel liked it or not.

The latter part of July 2004 was a strained period in Israeli-European relations, but not a unique one. The European vote at the UN came within days of Dutch foreign minister Bernard Bot's warning to Israel that further EU cooperation with Israel would depend on better cooperation from the Jewish state. At a signing ceremony marking Israel's full participation in the EU's Galileo satellite navigation project, Bot alluded that if Israel was not prepared to engage in a dialogue in a satisfactory way—especially over the construction

of the separation fence – then the EU would have to "consider possible con-
sequences."[25] The message was veiled, but the warning to Israel was clear.
The same week was witness to another public clash between France and
Israel, this time over Ariel Sharon's call to French Jews to move to Israel
immediately due to the wave of the "wildest anti-Semitism"[26] in France.
Sharon's comments caused a furor in France, leading French president
Jacques Chirac to declare that the Israeli prime minister would no longer be
a welcome guest in Paris until he explained his comments.

European criticism of the security fence is seen by many Israelis as reflective of an overall European antipathy to Israel and a lack of sensitivity for its
safety. Israelis have taken exception to European criticisms and to the lack
of understanding of the policy dilemmas facing Israel's leaders as they seek
to protect its citizens in the face of mounting terrorist and suicide bombing
attacks during the second Palestinian *intifada*. From an Israeli perspective,
European policies and attitudes are based on myths of "Palestinian victimiza-
tion" and Israeli power and its "excessive use of force."[27]

Israeli Settlements and the EU

European criticism of the security fence, even with the modifications to its
route, mirrors its opposition to the building of Israeli settlements in the West
Bank, namely that changing realities on the ground will render a two-state
solution impossible.[28] For Europe, Israeli settlement building, and especially
its unfettered expansion since 1993, is creating the geography of a single
state. European leaders have been consistent in their opposition to Israeli
settlements, seeing them as illegal under international law and as being in
contravention of the Fourth Geneva Convention, which prohibits an occu-
pying power from transferring its citizens from its own territory to occupied
territory. Israel's continued settlement building is viewed by European leaders as a sign of its bad faith and as undermining the prospects for peace. As
part of the first phase of the 2003 Roadmap drawn up by the Quartet, Israel
undertook to halt all settlement activity and dismantle settlement outposts
erected since March 2001. However, Israel has been ineffectual in keeping
to its commitment under the Roadmap, failing to remove the outposts and
implement a settlement freeze. Israel's continued settlement expansion is
seen as eroding trust, increasing Palestinian suffering and making the com-
promises Israel will need to make for peace more difficult. Following a tour
of East Jerusalem in January 2007, high representative Javier Solana told
reporters how he was shocked by the growth of settlements and the way the
security barrier was cutting into Palestinian land: "every time you go and

you see the situation [it gets] worse, the wall is more extended and settlements are more extended." Solana ended his remarks on a despairing note by, "*hoping* that these new realities would not prevent a two-state solution from happening."[29]

Israeli settlements have also been a source of an ongoing trade dispute between Israel and the EU. Under the 1995 Association Agreement, Israeli exports to the EU became exempt from custom duties. For European states, however, this exemption did not apply to goods produced in Israeli settlements since they fell outside the territorial scope of the EU-Israel trade agreement. In January 2002, the European commissioner for external affairs Chris Patten informed the European Parliament that "the EU must uphold the rule of law" on this issue. In December 2004, Israel eventually bowed to European pressure by agreeing to disclose the place of origin of all Israeli goods, and that goods from the settlements would no longer be marked as "made in Israel." This agreement did not remove the issue completely off the agenda. Toward the end of 2008, Great Britain called on the EU to be stricter in its application of this agreement and that such goods should be labeled clearly as originating from Israeli settlements rather than simply the West Bank.[30]

Israel, the EU and the al-Aqsa Intifada

The outbreak of the second *intifada* and Israel's response led to a new souring of Israeli-European relations. European leaders and civil society castigated Israel for its harsh measures in response to the Palestinian uprising. The majority of Europeans saw Ariel Sharon's visit to the Temple Mount/Haram al-Sharif in September 2000 and Israel's overreaction to the ensuing riots as triggering the escalation in violence. European leaders were particularly uneasy at what they saw as Israel's overreliance on, and excessive use of, military force, its destruction of Palestinian infrastructure, much of which had been financed by the EU and other donors, and the diplomatic isolation imposed on Yasser Arafat. Although European leaders condemned Palestinian attacks on Israeli citizens, they placed the onus on Israel to return to the negotiating table:

> Israel's security concerns are legitimate, but they must be addressed with full respect for human rights and within the framework of the rule of law. The EU urges Israel to put an immediate end to activities that are inconsistent with international humanitarian law and human rights, such as extra-judicial killings, to abstain from all acts of collective punishment such as demolition of Palestinian homes, to lift closures and curfews and to abstain from deportations of

family members. The EU firmly believes that there can be no justification for military actions directed indiscriminately against civilian neighbourhoods.[31]

Israel's decision to launch Operation Defensive Shield, an operation that began on 29 March 2002, during which the Israeli army reoccupied areas of the West Bank for the first time since conceding portions to the control of the Palestinian Authority under the Oslo Accords, was widely condemned by European leaders and European civil society. Commissioner Chris Patten warned Israel that its military operations were causing colossal damage to its reputation as a democracy. He went on to accuse Israel of trampling over "the rule of law, over the Geneva conventions, over what are generally regarded as [the] acceptable norms of behavior."[32] Many Europeans began to openly express doubts that Israel was truly interested in peace. In November 2003, for example, a Union-commissioned survey found that 59 percent of Europeans saw Israel as posing "the greatest threat to world peace."[33] Nearly 35 percent of Europeans polled believed that the Israel Defense Forces (IDF) intentionally targeted Palestinian civilians.[34] At the June 2002 Seville Council of Ministers meeting, European leaders laid out their position bluntly: "Military operations in the Occupied Territories must cease. Restrictions on freedom of movement must be lifted. Walls will not bring peace."[35]

From Disengagement to Annapolis

In December 2003 prime minister Ariel Sharon declared that he intended to dismantle Israeli settlements and withdraw unilaterally all Israeli military and civilian presence from Gaza and from areas in the northern part of the West Bank. At first, the EU was uncertain how to respond to Sharon's initiative, unclear of his long-term intentions. In February 2004, it offered a qualified support of Sharon's Disengagement Plan, so long as Israel's withdrawal from Gaza: took place in the context of the Roadmap and was a step toward a two-state solution; did not involve a transfer of settlement activity to the West Bank; there was a negotiated handover of responsibility to the Palestinian Authority; and Israel facilitated the rehabilitation and reconstruction of Gaza.[36] However, as the date of Israel's pullout from Gaza approached, European support became more pronounced, revealing a newfound respect for Ariel Sharon as he fended off domestic opposition to his plan. Israel completed its withdrawal from Gaza at the end of August 2005 as planned, though its withdrawal did not kick-start the peace process as many had hoped. Since the completion of Israel's withdrawal, Europe has begun to play a more pronounced role in helping to create the conditions for a revived Israeli-Palestinian negotiation process.

Monitoring the Gaza-Egyptian Border and Building Palestinian Security Capacity

The Gaza withdrawal led to Israel and the Palestinians signing an Agreement on Movement and Access (AMA) to and from Gaza in November 2005. This followed weeks of intense mediation by the U.S. with the assistance of the EU. As part of the agreement, Israel and the Palestinian Authority asked the EU to monitor the operations of the Rafah border crossing point on the Gaza-Egyptian border. The EU Border Assistance Mission (EUBAM Rafah) was established on 30 November 2005 for an initial duration of 12 months. The role of the mission was to monitor the performance of the Palestinian border control, security and customs officials working at the Rafah Terminal.[37] In May 2007, the mandate of the mission was extended until May 2008 and has since been extended again. Following Hamas' takeover of the Gaza Strip in June 2007, EUBAM's head of mission lieutenant general Pietro Pistolese declared a temporary suspension of operations at the Rafah crossing point. The EU monitors have since been inactive, having withdrawn their observers back to Israel. In January 2008, Hamas rejected the return of EUBAM observers to Rafah stating that the crossing point should be operated only by Palestinian and Egyptian forces. For its part, the EU holds that since the agreement was reached with Palestinian president Mahmoud Abbas and not with Hamas, its observers should return back to Rafah to resume the mission's activities as soon as the political situation in Gaza improves. For the time being, according to European sources, it is of little value in keeping all the members of the mission in the area and it is unclear how many observers of the original 87 members have actually remained in the region. Due to the situation on the ground, EU, Palestinian and Israeli officials do not expect that the Rafah crossing point will be opened on a permanent basis anytime soon. Nevertheless, following the 2009 war in Gaza, Javier Solana declared that the EU is "ready to return to Rafah and even to extend the mission . . . with monitors in Rafah and in other places."[38] Critics of EUBAM have argued that the monitoring mission was ineffectual, pointing out that it failed to stop the smuggling of weapons, goods and human beings across the Egyptian border. The symbolic and political significance of EUBAM was as important as its operational role. The setting up of EUBAM marked a significant step forward for Israeli-EU relations, insofar as it established a precedent whereby Israel agreed to give Europe a responsibility, albeit a limited one, within the "hard security" sphere.[39]

Since 2005, the EU has also been actively engaged in the rebuilding of Palestinian Authority security capacity through the European Union Police Mission for the Palestinian Territories (EUPOL-COPPS), based in Ramallah. The prime function of EUPOL-COPPS has been to enable the Palestinian Authority to take on greater responsibility for law and order in the Palestinian territories by improving its civil police and law enforcement capacity, and through the training of Palestinian police officers. In June 2008, under the German Presidency, the EU convened the Berlin conference in support of Palestinian Civil Security and Rule of Law which led to an expansion of the EUPOL-COPPS mandate to include a criminal justice component and by providing training to Palestinian judges, prosecutors and court administrators.

Rebuilding the Palestinian Economy

With the election of the Hamas-led government in January 2006, the EU, together with the other members of the Quartet, suspended all economic aid to the Palestinian Authority, until Hamas accepted three conditions: "non-violence, the recognition of Israel, and the acceptance of previous agreements and obligations." In May 2006, the Quartet addressed the economic impact of this step on the Palestinian economy by asking the EU to administer a "Temporary International Mechanism" (TIM), a mechanism designed to minimize the impact of the aid boycott on civilians by ensuring that that needs-based assistance could be delivered directly to the Palestinian people. TIM provided important relief. It paid some of the Palestinian fuel bills. It provided social allowances to almost 90 percent of non-security public sector employees. And it funded emergency assistance and food aid to some 73,000 low-income households.

As part of the Annapolis peace effort, the Palestinian prime minister, Salam Fayyad, announced a Palestinian Reform and Development Plan, a set of proposed reforms and budget priorities for the Palestinian economy. To support Fayyad's plan, international donors met in Paris in December 2007, the largest donor conference on the Palestinian issue in over a decade, and pledged over €5 billion. As in the Oslo years, the EU was again the major contributor. In 2007 the EU provided €550 million in financial assistance, and when bilateral assistance from member states is included, the total European assistance to the Palestinians was close to €1 billion for that year. In early 2008, the EU replaced TIM with a new mechanism PEGASE (Mécanisme Palestino-Européen de Gestion de l'Aide Socio-Economique). PEGASE is designed to work more closely with the PA by widening the focus of EU financial assistance to include development assistance, though this assistance will only be provided to the West Bank and not to Gaza.[40]

Conclusion: From Divergence to Convergence

The question of European positions and its potential role in the Israeli-Palestinian peace process has bedeviled Israeli-European relations. The divide between Israel and Europe over the resolution of the Arab-Israeli conflict runs much deeper than disagreements over specific practices and immediate events. Israel and the EU hold a fundamentally differing set of priorities, interests, and strategies toward the conflict. It is those differences and not just policy disagreements that have brought Israel and Europe to loggerheads over the years. Recent years have witnessed, however, a convergence of European and Israeli views and strategies toward a resolution of the Israeli-Palestinian conflict. This convergence has been driven by a number of factors.

First, the majority of Israelis and Europeans now hold a shared vision regarding the contours of a resolution to the Israeli-Palestinian conflict, namely the creation of a Palestinian state. Israeli politicians have begun to talk openly of the corrupting influence on Israeli society of its occupation of Palestinian land and of the necessity of a Palestinian state as a guarantor of Israel's long-term survival as a democratic Jewish state. Former prime minister Ehud Olmert even warned that the failure to reach a peace agreement could plunge Israel into a South African–style apartheid struggle, a view long held by many Europeans.

Second, such an outcome can only emerge through a process of negotiation and by generating the necessary socio-economic and security environment for both reaching and implementing an Israeli-Palestinian agreement. This involves developing strategies to reinforce the standing of Palestinian president Mahmoud Abbas, the development of reform programs to reinvigorate the Palestinian economy and the rebuilding of the capacity of Palestinian security forces to maintain law and order in the Palestinian territories. Here, the EU is seen as an important partner in this task. Equally there has been a marked change in Israeli thinking of the potential value of a more robust international third-party presence in overseeing the process of Palestinian reform and in monitoring any agreements reached with the Palestinians.[41] Israel has looked to Europe with a greater appreciation of its experience and its capacity to fulfill such roles.

Third, the exclusion of Hamas from the political process. European governments have been steadfast in their support of president Mahmoud Abbas and in their economic and diplomatic boycott of Hamas. The EU did welcome the Mecca agreement leading to the formation of a Palestinian national unity government in March 2007 and expressed its readiness to work with, and to resume its assistance to, a legitimate Palestinian government. But it qualified this support by insisting that the government adopt "a platform reflecting the Quartet principles," namely the recognition of Israel, the renouncing of violence and the acceptance of past agreements signed between both parties, that is, the Oslo Accords. There have been a number of growing dissenting voices in Europe questioning the policy of isolating Hamas, and calling on Europe be more engaged in the process of Palestinian reconciliation by bringing Hamas into the political process.[42] But this has not resulted yet in any European policy initiative to engage directly with Hamas.

Finally, Europe has adopted a strategy of a more direct engagement with Israel (and the Palestinians) on the peace process. Europe has remained forthright in its condemnation of specific Israeli policies: the continuation of settlement building, the construction of the separation fence/wall, and the deteriorating humanitarian conditions in Gaza. Yet it has matched those criticisms with a concerted commitment to work at upgrading relations at the bilateral level and to conduct a strategic dialogue with Israel not just on the peace process but also on shared strategic concerns such as the Iranian threat, counterterrorism and organized crime. In addition, the EU has pledged to help Israel integrate into UN agencies and talked of the need to include Israeli experts in EU peacekeeping forces.

By the end of 2008, tensions over the peace process appeared to have receded into the background. Israel and the EU had seemingly found a common ground over issues of representation, process and outcome with regard to the Israeli-Palestinian conflict and the potential contribution of the EU in bringing the conflict to an end. The decision by European foreign ministers in Luxembourg in June 2008 to upgrade relations signaled a new phase in Israeli-European relations.[43] Experience from the past shows that slippage in the Israeli-Palestinian peace process can easily result in the unraveling of any Israeli-EU rapprochement. The Israeli military invasion of Gaza in December 2008 and its economic blockade of Gaza quickly brought Israel and the EU back to loggerheads with each other. Exchanges took on a familiar tone of accusation and recrimination. All talk of an upgrade was placed on hold until Israel not only reaffirmed its commitment to the creation of a Palestinian state but also took substantive measures to that effect.[44] It is uncertain to what extent the current disagreements between Israel and the EU will lead to a further of unraveling of Israeli-EU relations and what this might bode for the future development of Israeli-EU relations. This is a theme that we will return to in the concluding chapter of the book.

CHAPTER TWO

~

Israeli–European Union Relations in a Multilateral Context

"There is nothing more difficult to take in hand, more perilous to conduct, or more uncertain in its success, than to take the lead in a new order of things."

—Niccolo Machiavelli, 1532

During the last thirty years, the Arab-Israeli conflict has defined the contours of Israeli-European relations. Israel has viewed European positions on the conflict as inimical to its security and as reflecting uncritically the positions of the Arab world. European criticisms of Israeli actions and policies are increasingly interpreted by Israel as proof of European bias for the Arab cause and of a general hostility among Europeans toward Israel. Accordingly, as discussed in the previous chapter, Israel has sought to limit any direct role played by Europe in the Arab-Israeli peace process. At the same time, Israel and the EU have over the past twenty years been engaged in a series of multilateral initiatives in which Europe has been directly responsible for the management of relations between Israel and the Arab world. This chapter will discuss the role the EU has played in three multilateral initiatives: The Multilateral Arab-Israeli Talks, the Euro-Mediterranean Partnership (the Barcelona Process), and the Union for the Mediterranean. The role of the EU in each of these multilateral fora, and its (in)ability to contain the impact of the Arab-Israeli conflict on these efforts to develop new collaborative security structures, has affected Israeli confidence in the EU as a political actor and Israeli perceptions toward the EU.

27

Israel, Europe and the Multilateral Arab-Israeli Peace Talks

With the end of the Gulf war in the summer of 1991, international efforts to re-launch the Arab-Israeli peace process were intensified. Given the reinvigorated role that the Security Council and the UN in general had played in lending legitimacy to the military actions undertaken to restore Kuwait's sovereignty there were high hopes within European quarters that an international conference on the Middle East peace process, under the auspices of the UN, would be convened, and that the EC would play a key role in the next phase of the peace process. These hopes proved to be short-lived. Neither the Security Council, nor the UN at large, was to play any role in the political developments engendered by the Gulf war. The United States took it upon itself to set up an institutional framework to deal with the Arab-Israeli conflict and effectively blocked any alternative international efforts. While Madrid played host, and gave its name, to the conference convened by the United States at the end of October 1991, such was the distrust of Europe by Israel that the EC was offered only a minor role in the proceedings. Indeed, America turned to Moscow, rather than Europe, to act as co-sponsor to the Madrid conference, despite the fact that the Soviet Union's power was visibly declining and that it was on the verge of collapse. Nor was the EC offered any role in the bilateral negotiations that followed the Madrid conference. Instead, Europe was consigned to operating solely within the framework of five working groups of the multilateral talks set up by the Madrid conference.

The multilateral talks were to run in parallel with the bilateral negotiations. The aim was to bring together Israel, its immediate Arab neighbors and the wider circle of Arab states in the Maghreb and the Gulf to address issues of regional and mutual concern. While the bilateral talks were to concentrate on the political issues of territorial control and sovereignty, border demarcations, security arrangements and the political rights of the Palestinians, the multilaterals would examine a range of economic, social and environmental issues which extend across national boundaries, the resolution of which are a prerequisite for long-term regional development and peace in the Middle East. The idea of the multilateral track was grounded in a functionalist, liberalist conception of international cooperation and peace according to which the enmeshing of the states in the region in an ever-widening web of economic, technical and welfare interdependencies would force them to set aside their political and/or ideological rivalries. The process of continuing cooperation in areas of mutual concern would blur long-held animosities and create a new perception of shared needs. Continuous interaction would be accompanied by a learning process which would foster a fundamental change in attitudes and lead to a convergence of expectations and the institutionalization of new norms of behavior.

The broadening of the peace process through the inclusion of a multilateral framework was dismissed by many as simply a way of placating Israel, thereby ensuring its participation in the Madrid conference. Moreover, the creation of this track was dismissed by European states which saw it as a poor consolation for their exclusion from the sponsorship of the Madrid conference and the substantive issues under discussion in the bilateral negotiations. There was little expectation that the multilateral talks would make any significant contribution to the promotion of peace between Israel and the Arab world.

The EU was entrusted with the running of the Regional Economic Development Working Group (REDWG), the largest of the five working groups, and the one that reflected most fully the broader goals of the multilateral track.[1] Such was the distrust of Europe by Israel at the time of the Madrid conference that it insisted that European states be excluded from the deliberations of the Arms Control and Regional Security (ACRS) working group which was led by the United States. Given the antipathy of the Europeans to the multilateral talks, it was of no surprise that the initial meetings of the REDWG working group, held in Brussels (May 1992), Paris (October 1992) and Rome (May 1993), failed to discuss anything substantive. Europe (and Israel) invested few diplomatic resources in those meetings. The discussions for the most part revolved around procedural issues and, in particular, the representation of the Palestinian delegation. Formally, the early meetings established a working agenda and areas of work were delegated to various European states. But little financial support was provided to support these activities and little headway was made in the first two years of the multilaterals.[2]

The fourth round of talks took place in Copenhagen in November 1993 shortly after the signing of the Declaration of Principles between Israel and the Palestinians. The breakthrough between Israel and the PLO led to a marked transformation in Israeli-European relations in both tone and substance. Israel began to lavish praise on Europe, seeing it as a model for putting aside past hatreds and for building new cooperative structures for peace and stability. Shimon Peres' vision of a "new Middle East" drew direct parallels with Europe's experience in the aftermath of the Second World War. The multilateral track of the peace process gained a new relevance. In light of the breakthrough at the bilateral level there was an overwhelming recognition in Copenhagen of the need to intensify the workings of REDWG to ensure that its activities would not become marginalized. Accordingly the group adopted the Copenhagen Action Plan, which outlined thirty-three different ventures. In order to finance these activities, the EU announced that it would allocate $9.2 million for the preparation of studies and the running of inter-sessional activities to ensure the rapid implementation of the Copenhagen Action Plan.

The EU, with the support of Israel, began to take the lead in encouraging the regional parties to explore ideas about the future long-term nature of their economic relations, and to develop a vision of potential institutional mechanisms and frameworks to sustain their efforts toward regional cooperation. At the plenary meeting in Rabat (held in June 1994), the regional parties agreed upon a number of guidelines and principles to steer their work in the future. Specifically, they recognized the need for: (i) the pooling of common capacities and the joint tackling of common problems through coordinated efforts; (ii) the removing of obstacles to a more prominent role for the private sector; (iii) the promotion of regional trade, the facilitating of investment and the development of infrastructure; and (iv) the encouragement of the free flow of people, goods, services, capital and information within the region. The working group also agreed in Rabat to establish a smaller monitoring committee which would be staffed by parties from the region. The aim in setting up this committee was to allow the core regional parties—Egypt, Israel, Jordan and the Palestinians—to take a more direct role in implementing the Copenhagen Action Plan, organizing the various sectoral activities, developing a set of priorities and identifying future projects for the working group. It was also agreed that the committee would be jointly chaired by the core regional participants and by the EU. The regional parties' co-chairmanship would be held for six months and would rotate alphabetically, with Egypt assuming the chair on 1 January 1995. The specific work of the monitoring committee was divided among four sectoral committees whose membership was confined to the four core regional parties. The chairing of these committees was shared out, with Egypt taking on responsibility for work on finance and Israel for trade; Jordan was placed in charge of promoting regional infrastructure, while the Palestinians chaired the committee on tourism.

With the establishment of the Monitoring Committee, it was quickly recognized that a new secretariat was needed to help manage such a broad and extensive program of activities and to be effective it needed to be located in the region. It was also decided to appoint an executive secretary, provided by the EU, and staffed by personnel from the region, to service the work of the monitoring committee and the four sectoral committees. Reaching agreement among the regional parties on the permanent location of the secretariat proved to be much harder, and it was not until the Amman Economic summit in November 1995 that the parties agreed it would be based permanently in Amman. In practice, however, the secretariat, with a skeleton staff, had been operating out of Amman since March 1995 servicing a series of regional meetings and workshops aimed at promoting regional economic cooperation. Although embryonic in its nature and functioning, the secretariat was reflective of a move toward fashioning new common structures of cooperation, coordination and decision making in the Middle East. It was the first, and only, functioning regional institution that was spawned by the Middle East peace process in which Egyptian, Israeli, Jordanian and Palestinian officials worked together on a daily basis with the active and ongoing support of the EU.

The multilaterals were short-lived and came to an end in 1996 when the Arab states formally suspended their participation in protest over the impasse in negotiations on the redeployment of Israeli troops from Hebron. They were never resumed. But the demise of the multilaterals had begun well prior to the election of Binyamin Netanyahu as Israeli prime minister in May 1996 and the subsequent slowdown in the peace process. The multilateral talks suffered from a number of structural weaknesses. As the talks moved from the stage where ideas for future cooperation were raised and discussed to the point where decisions were actually reached and projects implemented, it was inevitable that conflicts of interest would emerge and disagreements would arise. Those disagreements—and in particular the nascent rivalry between Israel and Egypt—began to dominate the proceedings and ultimately stifled the activities of the multilateral working groups.

From the outset, the multilateral talks suffered from differing expectations and varying interests of the parties. They offered Israel the opportunity to break out of its regional isolation. The talks were seen by Israel as a vehicle for the normalization of its position in the Middle East and for the development of bilateral ties with countries of the Gulf and North Africa. But Israel's interests were much more ambitious. Israel's leaders, most notably Shimon Peres, spoke of the emergence of a new regional order in the Middle East wherein Israel would play a central role. Such talk of a reshaping of the existing order led to fears in the Arab world of Israel's intention to establish economic hegemony over the region. Most notably, Egypt regarded the end of Israel's isolation and the potential new order as a direct threat to its regional standing and interests. Although the Oslo peace process gave Egypt legitimacy for its own peace treaty with Israel, Egypt was intent from the outset on limiting progress in the multilateral talks and on containing Israel's influence. The potential political and economic benefits accruing for

Israel from the process of normalization in the region was seen in Cairo as undercutting Egypt's influence and power.

Tensions between Israel and Egypt came to the surface primarily in meetings of the ACRS working group in which the Europeans were bystanders. But the friction between Israel and Egypt was not confined solely to discussions within ACRS and also affected the deliberations of the REDWG, coming to a head over the location of the REDWG secretariat and the negotiations over the creation of a Middle East and North Africa Development Bank (MENABANK). Egypt saw itself as the cornerstone of sustainable economic cooperation in the region and was determined to control the pace of normalization and economic engagement with Israel. At the second Middle East and North Africa (MENA) Economic summit, held in Amman in October 1995 (see below), Egyptian foreign minister Amr Mousa publicly berated other Arab states for rushing to normalize their relations with Israel. Egypt was particularly wary of any initiatives that might marginalize its economic interests.

The demise of the multilaterals cannot be attributed solely to Arab reluctance to engage with Israel. Israel was more interested in utilizing the multilaterals as a means of developing bilateral ties with the Arab world than with truly developing new multilateral cooperative ventures. It also overplayed the issue of normalization by sending large, high-profile delegations to the plenary sessions hosted by Gulf and Maghreb states, primarily intended for domestic consumption. With the election of Binyamin Netanyahu as prime minister in May 1996, Israel lost all interest in the multilaterals. Netanyahu ridiculed Shimon Peres' vision of a "new Middle East" as naïve and illusory and saw little Israeli interest in maintaining these talks. More significantly, Israel turned its attention away from the multilateral talks toward a new multilateral process launched within the context of the Madrid peace process, namely the convening of the MENA Economic summits.

In October 1994 a new multilateral economic process, the MENA Economic summits, was launched in Casablanca, Morocco. While this process was technically distinct from REDWG, in reality the two processes overlapped, particularly because many of the same officials from the region were active. However, unlike REDWG, the primary objective of the MENA process was to engage the private sector in regional economic development rather than relying solely on government resources. Despite persistent concerns about Israeli economic dominance, the MENA summits enhanced a sense of shared regional interests among Arabs and Israelis in attracting private sector investment. The summits also led to a commitment to create three new economic institutions: a Regional Business Council; a Middle East and Mediterranean Travel and Tourism Association (MEMTTA); and most significantly, a Middle East Development Bank.

The introduction of the MENA Economic summits, and the attention these summits attracted, cast a large shadow over the multilaterals. Israel sent a delegation of nearly 400 people to the first meeting. As with the Madrid conference, the Europeans were excluded in the planning of these economic summits. The Europeans felt the Americans had usurped their only role in the peace process by taking the initiative out of REDWG and had created a parallel, and in their view competitive, economic process based on new regional institutions dominated by the Americans. In particular, they were strongly opposed to the establishment of the Middle East Development Bank, much to the annoyance of Israel who had initiated this idea. The Europeans opposed the idea of the bank on economic grounds—particularly given the sufficient sources for loans to the region and the financial burdens of financing what they perceived as a redundant institution. Yet the Europeans harbored political doubts that went beyond the economics of the bank. In short, the Europeans complained that the United States could not continue to control the political agenda of the region while insisting the Europeans foot the bill. At Casablanca, German and French officials (speaking for the EU) objected to the bank, arguing it would amount "to American control over European money." Britain, France, and Germany continued to express opposition to the bank and instead promoted a proposal calling for a Middle East and North Africa Financial Intermediation Organization (MENAFIO) that would promote political cooperation, economic coordination, and resource mobilization but which would not have its own capital.[3]

The multilaterals also suffered from a failure of political leadership and commitment. From the outset the EU saw its participation in the multilaterals as a way of being sidelined by the Americans and Israel from any substantive engagement in the bilateral negotiations. Accordingly, the EU concentrated its efforts on the development of its own regional initiative, the Euro-Mediterranean Partnership (the Barcelona Process) which it launched in 1995 and saw little reason to encourage the Arab states to re-engage in the multilateral talks.

Israel, Europe, and the Euro-Mediterranean Partnership—The Barcelona Process

In November 1995, the EU launched in Barcelona the "Euro-Mediterranean Partnership" (EMP)—the "Barcelona Process" (BP)—with the aim of redefining its relations with the Mediterranean states on its southern periphery and of developing a new framework for peaceful and cooperative relations in the Mediterranean region. While the Barcelona Process built on the various Mediterranean policies developed by the EU since the 1960s, it also marked at the same time a radical departure from those policies, in that it sought to create a more integrated set of relationships than those engendered simply by the bilateral customs agreements and financial protocols of the 1970s and 1980s. It sought to create a new regional framework for future relations between the EU and the poorer states of the southern Mediterranean. What the EU envisioned in Barcelona was no less than the creation of a "stability pact," which would situate economic development and trade relations in the broader context of Mediterranean security.

The launching of the Barcelona Process was an ambitious exercise. Borrowing from the experience of the Commisssion on Security and Co-operation in Europe (CSCE), the declaration signed in Barcelona in November 1995 outlined three broad objectives: (i) to strengthen political dialogue on a regular basis with the eventual aim of establishing a common area of peace and stability, including respect for human rights and democracy; (ii) the creation of a shared zone of prosperity through the establishment of a free trade area and a substantial increase in financial support from the EU to attend to the social and economic challenges which come with transition; (iii) the development of an active civil society and the promotion of understanding between different cultures and exchanges at the level of civil society.

The driving force behind the launching of the Barcelona Process was the belief that the root causes of instability in the Mediterranean region were economic underdevelopment and social inequality, and that these issues needed to be tackled collectively within a multilateral framework. Economic incentives remained the main tool in the hands of the EU in dealing with the potential security threats arising from its southern shores, but they would be complemented by political dialogue and extensive cooperation in social and cultural affairs. Enhanced economic cooperation through the creation of a free trade zone in the Mediterranean region by 2010 would be accompanied by the development of a new set of cooperative frameworks for future political, security and civil relations.

The underlying assumptions and approach of the Barcelona Process mirrored the creation of the multilateral talks and reflected the increasingly prevalent approach of "cooperative security," namely that of addressing security from more than just a military perspective. Although the military dimension of security and the potential for inter-state conflict were not totally overlooked in the Barcelona declaration, stability in the Mediterranean region was now widened to include a broad range of issues such as internal disintegration, migration flows, environmental degradation, human rights and economic development.

The thinking behind the Barcelona Process rested on a number of assumptions. First and foremost was the understanding of a common Euro-Mediterranean space and the idea that the states of this geo-political region shared a common set of interests, concerns and values. In order to fulfill the ambitious and wide-ranging agenda laid out in the Barcelona declaration, it would require a radical change in the domestic, foreign and security policies of the southern Mediterranean partner states, and the putting aside of long-held rivalries. It also demanded a significant transformation in their domestic and economic policies, and in their conception of civil society. It would require a transformation in their perceptions of their own identity and self-definition, in their regional identity and in their conception of threat and security, as well as the opening up of economic and trade relations with each other. In this respect, it was assumed that the southern Mediterranean states would invest in the "Euro-Mediterranean region" and would regard it as their natural geopolitical space, that they would see security and economic issues as intrinsically linked with the fortunes of the Euro-Mediterranean Partnership.

Israel and the Barcelona Process

The decision by the EU to include Israel as a member of the Barcelona Process, which would now locate its relations with Israel within a regional and Mediterranean context, represented a radical departure from previous European policies. It was based on the assumption that a fundamental change in Arab-Israeli relations had occurred and that the Arab states of the EMP were now prepared to accept Israel as an equal and legitimate partner and that they would be willing to engage with Israel in a new set of multilateral ventures at the regional level.

Israel's response to the Barcelona Process was mixed. Europe's vision for the Mediterranean and its focus on bringing about socio-economic change and building new frameworks of regional cooperation mirrored Shimon Peres' vision of a "new Middle East." Israel saw the launching of the Barcelona Process as an important step in the peace process in that it promoted regional confidence building measures and provided an environment in which Israel could develop its relationships with the countries of North Africa. At the time of the launching of the Barcelona Process in November 1995 Israel was more open to Europe playing an enhanced role in promoting Arab-Israeli reconciliation.

At the same time, many in Israel viewed Europe's agenda in the Mediterranean, namely the fear of instability in North Africa and illegal migration, as of little concern to Israel. Others, especially those in the Ministry of Finance, saw little financial gain from Israel's involvement in the Barcelona Process. Israel objected that the EU considered it as one of the southern Mediterranean countries, and that Israeli-European economic relations would now be located within a Mediterranean framework. Israel was especially surprised to discover that its 1995 Association Agreement was labeled as a "Euro-Mediterranean Agreement" and had been classified as an instrument of the Barcelona Process. Israel saw its economic place as being in Europe and not in the Mediterranean. Economically speaking, Israel would have preferred to have been included on the European side of the equation and to have spoken of a relationship between "16" and "11" states, rather than the divide of 15 EU member states and the 12 southern Mediterranean partners. In short, viewed from Israel, the Barcelona Process undermined the economic logic and the special status that the EU Council of Ministers had accorded Israel the previous year at the December 1994 Essen summit.[4]

Israel was uncomfortable with the Mediterranean region-building logic of the Barcelona Process. Even though Israel is a "Euro-Mediterranean society in the making," the country has always perceived the Mediterranean as a place of "otherness" that has been tainted by the ongoing Arab-Israeli conflict.[5] The Mediterranean as a region had not figured among Israeli foreign policy preoccupations nor been included in its official discourse. Prior to the Barcelona Process, Israel did not seriously consider itself as being part of the Mediterranean. Even after the launch of the EMP, discussions in Israel on the "Mediterranean option" were seen as exotic and remained confined to a relatively small group of Israeli academics, politicians and intellectuals.[6]

Above all, there was concern in Israel that despite its assertions to the contrary, Europe would exploit the Barcelona Process in order to gain influence in the Arab-Israeli peace process. With long-standing Israeli suspicions about Europe's neutrality and its pro-Arab tendencies, there was a fear that the Euro-Mediterranean meetings would develop into a forum where Israel would be outnumbered and besieged. The EU stressed that the EMP should be seen as a separate framework. The EMP was intended to complement and not compete with the Arab-Israeli peace process. Indeed, the Barcelona declaration states that "this Euro-Mediterranean initiative is not intended to replace the other activities and initiatives undertaken in the interest of peace, stability and development of the region, but it will contribute to their success." The distinction between the Barcelona Process and the Middle East peace process was rhetorical. From the outset the fortunes of the two processes were clearly intertwined. The EU had given little thought to how it intended to prevent any potential setbacks in the Arab-Israeli peace process from spilling over and affecting the Barcelona Process, and to whether it possessed the capacity to mediate those potential crises within the Barcelona framework. Equally, it was unclear whether Israel and the Arab states would look to Europe to play such a role and if they would use the Barcelona Process to overcome their differences and become a forum for the promotion of confidence building measures.

It took little time for the tensions between Israel and Egypt to spill over into the meetings of the Barcelona Process. From the outset, difficulties emerged in determining the agenda for the meetings on political and security cooperation. All proposals put forward by the Europeans were immediately vetoed by the Arab states, which despite putting their signatures to the Barcelona declaration, were not prepared to cooperate with Israel on matters related to security and confidence building measures. Furthermore, the Arab states were unwilling to host any of the meetings in this area because of the participation of Israel. Just as many of the Arab countries had agreed to participate in the multilateral talks at the behest of the United States, so Arab participation in the Barcelona Process was related more to the furthering of their bilateral interests with Europe than to their eagerness to engage with Israel in cooperative ventures at the regional level.

The original intention was to hold the follow-up second Euro-Mediterranean ministerial conference in Tunis. However, fears that the stalled Arab-Israeli peace process would jeopardize the proceedings led to the meeting being moved to Valetta, Malta. This deflected the problem but did not remove it entirely and the faltering peace process dominated the proceedings anyway. By the time of the meeting in Valetta, the context of the peace process had changed significantly. The wave of terrorists' attacks within Israel in early 1996 had led to the election in May 1996 of a center-right-wing government led by Binyamin Netanyahu and to the demise of the peace process. The decision of the new Israeli government to open the Hasmonean Tunnel in the Old City of Jerusalem in September 1996 had led to widespread rioting in the West Bank, resulting in the deaths of 64 Palestinians and 15 Israeli soldiers. At the end of 1996, in response to the deteriorating situation and the impasse in negotiations over the redeployment of Israeli troops from Hebron as stipulated in the Oslo II Accords, the Arab countries announced that they would be suspending their participation in the multilateral talks. Relations between Israel and the Palestinians reached a crisis point in February 1997 with the decision of the Israeli government to start building new homes for Jewish residents in Har Homa/Jabal Abu Ghneim in East Jerusalem. This action brought the peace process to a total standstill and all contact between the Israeli government and the Palestinian Authority was suspended.

Keeping the problems of the peace process out of the Barcelona deliberations was only possible if there was reason to believe that those problems were short term. Given the breakdown of the peace process, it was not surprising that this issue cast a shadow over the deliberations leading up to the meeting in Valetta. Virtually all preparation of documentation relating to the political and security chapters of the Barcelona declaration was paralyzed. The Arab states were adamant that any arrangements and outcomes of the Malta meeting that might be construed as security-related cooperation with Israel be sidestepped. For their part, European officials went out of their way to stress that they did not want the Malta meeting to be dominated by the crisis in Israeli-Palestinian relations. "We intend to make sure that the Euro-Mediterranean relationship is the focus of the meeting," an aide to a European commissioner insisted. "We will not let our relationship with these countries become hostage to the Middle East peace process."[7]

At the same time, the focus of Europe's priorities in the Mediterranean had shifted since the launching of the Barcelona Process. European leaders had become alarmed by the turn of events. They felt that they could no longer stand idly aside and watch the Middle East slide into a new cycle of violence. In a declaration issued by the Council of Ministers, the Europeans announced their intention of becoming more directly involved in efforts to restart negotiations. In a speech to the third MENA Economic summit held in Cairo in October 1996, the Irish foreign minister informed the participants: "[The EU] has a *responsibility both to the region and to itself* (our italics) to put the Peace Process back on track."[8] As a sign of its determination to revive the moribund peace process and to adopt a more proactive approach, the EU decided shortly after to create the new post of a special envoy to the Middle East peace process.

Accordingly the EU approached the meeting in Valetta with two main priorities: (i) to strengthen the EMP; and (ii) to renew contacts between Israel and the Palestinian Authority. European officials continued to disavow any linkage between the Barcelona Process and Middle East peace process. Such statements were not matched, however, by their actions. The two-day meeting was dominated by the question of the Middle East peace process and the intense efforts by European officials to bring about a meeting between the president of the Palestinian Authority, Yasser Arafat, and Israel's foreign minister, David Levy, during the conference. That those two leaders did meet—the first high-level contact between the two sides since Israel's decision to start building new homes in Har Homa/Jabal Abu Ghneim in

East Jerusalem in February—was heralded as a great success and testimony to Europe's capacity to bring Israel and the Palestinians together. However, the focus on trying to resurrect the Arab-Israel peace process during the Malta conference pushed the wider agenda of the EMP to the sidelines. The extensive mediation undertaken, and the attention this effort attracted, meant that the fortunes of the Middle East peace process now took center stage. From this point on, the ebb and flow of the peace process dominated all efforts to push the agenda of the Barcelona Process forward.

At Malta, the Middle East peace process and the Barcelona Process became entwined. Thereafter, it became impossible for the EU to separate future progress in the Barcelona Process from the fortunes of the Middle East peace process. The future of sectoral cooperation in the Mediterranean became hostage to the fortunes of peace in the Middle East. The Arab states refused to hold meetings of the process in their countries because of the presence of Israel and even tried to convene meetings without informing Israel. Arab unwillingness to sit down with Israel to discuss joint ventures and cooperative projects led to a Euro-Mediterranean ministerial conference on industrial cooperation, scheduled for the end of October 1997 in Marrakech, Morocco, as part of the EMP, being canceled. In an effort to get the process moving, the EU even asked Israel to assume a lower profile. For example, in a meeting on the potential for financial partnerships in London in March 1998, where partner countries were to be represented at the ministerial level, the EU asked Israel not to send its minister of finance, Ya'akov Ne'eman. Israel refused to comply with this request, and the minister eventually participated in all of the meetings.[9]

Progress in the Barcelona Process could no longer remain separate from the Middle East peace process. The speed of progress in the Barcelona Process had now become dependent on events beyond its immediate influence, namely the peace process. The Euro-Mediterranean Partnership had become, as one European statement crudely put it, "contaminated by the peace process."[10] The impact was most pronounced in the first basket of the Barcelona Process which was aimed at building a new political security relationship in the Mediterranean and at drafting a "Mediterranean Charter for Peace and Stability." A report produced by the EuroMeSCo network on political and security cooperation in the Mediterranean concluded that "the persistence of a number of long standing conflicts, particularly the conflict in the Middle East . . . make the early implementation of military and military-related Confidence Building Measures (CBMs) and Confidence and Security Building Measures (CSBMs) difficult." It continued: "The resolution of the Middle

East peace process is a precondition for the implementation of a fully-fledged area of peace and stability in the overall Mediterranean environment."[11]

The early meetings of the Senior Officials Committee on the Political and Security Partnership focused on developing a series of arms control concepts for the region and a set of CSBMs. Sidetracked by the Middle East peace process, the Malta ministerial meeting was unable to find a consensus on steps to be taken in the political and security chapter and the meeting failed to endorse three documents that were intended to guide policy in the security realm: (i) a plan of action; (ii) an inventory of CSBMs; (iii) guidelines and principles outlining an avenue toward a Mediterranean Charter for Peace and Stability.[12]

Little progress was made at the third ministerial meeting in Stuttgart in the area of political and security cooperation and the drawing up of a Mediterranean Charter for Peace and Stability. While areas for discussion were drawn up and general principles were agreed upon, no concrete measures were settled upon by the participants. The ministers instructed the senior officials to go away and prepare a provisional text for the charter by the informal ministerial conference, which was to be held under the Portuguese Presidency in May 2000 in Lisbon. The external relations commissioner Chris Patten stated in December 1999 that the charter "is expected to be approved during the second half of year 2000, [and] will provide Europe with a lasting role in the maintenance of peace and stability in the region."

However, no time frame was established for the signing of the charter at the Stuttgart conference, only an understanding that it would be signed according to a European Commission report, "as soon as political circumstances allow i.e. when *sufficient* (our italics) progress has been made in the Middle East peace."[13] The report failed to elaborate what sufficient progress would entail in practice. Little progress was made after Stuttgart.

The position of the Arab states concerning any continued discussion of the charter, and its adoption, is best summarized by Fathy El Shazly:

> It was widely believed among Arabs that no process entitled peace and stability could be embarked upon between partners while some of them were legally in a state of war. Arabs also believed that military and security building measures under those conditions would practically amount to bestowing blessing and tolerance on the foreign occupation of Arab territories. Therefore, the following understanding was reached among Arabs: (i) it would be very difficult to accept military measures as long as foreign occupation persisted; (ii) necessary time should be allowed for the reflection on and drafting of the Charter, with

the hope that by the time it will be ripe for implementation peace could have finally been achieved in the Middle East.[14]

At the next ministerial meeting held in Marseilles in November 2000, the hopes of the French Presidency that the charter might come into force were dashed by the boycott of that meeting by Syria and Lebanon. The meeting decided to "defer the adoption of the Charter *due to the political context* (our italics)."[15] By the time of the Valencia gathering in April 2002, hopes for making any further progress on the charter had all but disappeared. The concluding remarks of the Presidency made no reference to the charter. Similarly, the "Valencia Action Plan" approved by the meeting confines to a single sentence future work on the charter. The conference agreed "to confirm the mandate of the senior officials on the Draft Charter for Peace and Stability to continue their work *as appropriate* (our italics) so as to enable the Charter to be adopted as soon as the political situation allows."[16]

With the further deterioration of the situation in the Middle East, the gatherings of the foreign ministers within the Barcelona framework began to focus more on the immediate diplomatic efforts to contain the violence and restart negotiations than on the long-term aims of the EMP. The meetings became a forum wherein the Arab states sought to attack Israel and garner the support of the Europeans. By the time of the meeting in Valencia in April 2002, the escalating violence between Israel and the Palestinians dominated much of the proceedings. Nearly half of the conclusions delivered at the end of the meeting addressed the issue of the crisis in the Middle East, with but only a single sentence devoted to the Charter for Peace and Stability.

The EU maintained consistently that the Barcelona Process and the Middle East peace process should be viewed as two distinct processes. It expressed disappointment and regret that the difficulties in the peace process limited progress within the Barcelona framework. Yet not only did Europe fail to contain rivalry between Israel and the Arab states and prevent it from affecting the agenda of the Barcelona Process, but as has been shown, through its own policies it contributed to the conflation of the two processes. Faced with recurrent stalemate in the peace process since 1996, the EU was determined to play a more active political role in the Arab-Israeli peace process. As a result, the Middle East peace process was defined, de facto, by the EU as an integral part of its Mediterranean policy. Not surprisingly, this added to the distrust of Europe in Israel and was a contributing factor in the marked deterioration in Israeli-European relations during those years.

The Union for the Mediterranean (UfM)

In July 2008 Euro-Mediterranean heads of state and government launched in Paris the "Union for the Mediterranean" (UfM).[17] The UfM aimed at providing a new political impetus to the faltering Euro-Mediterranean Partnership through creating a new framework that would offer greater co-ownership to the southern Mediterranean partners. The idea of the UfM first came to light during Nicolas Sarkozy's campaign for the French Presidency. Sarkozy's envisioned a new "Mediterranean Union" through which Europe would conduct its relations with Turkey, which he described during his campaign as a "great Mediterranean country," and the Arab world at large. It would also offer a framework for finding a solution to the Israeli-Palestinian conflict as well as attend to the problem of immigration, cultural diversity, trade and development issues with the Mediterranean region. Sarkozy's project was based on four central ideas: (i) the UfM would strengthen France's role as a major player in the Mediterranean; (ii) the Mediterranean had become insignificant in the global economy; (iii) all EU policies, especially the Barcelona Process, toward its Mediterranean neighbors had failed; (iv) the UfM would re-launch the debate regarding the Mediterranean's geo-strategic significance. But, above all, Sarkozy's Mediterranean vision was driven by domestic concerns, namely that continued instability in the Mediterranean southern shores would eventually affect France.

Sarkozy's initial vision of a UfM encountered considerable resistance from other EU member states, especially Germany. The European Commission also opposed the idea, seeing it as undermining the EMP. Italy and Spain were the first countries to express their concern. In December 2007, the Italian and Spanish prime ministers reached an agreement with France that Sarkozy's vision would not endanger other EU policies toward the Mediterranean region, namely the Barcelona Process. Yet the strongest opposition to the project came from Germany. Chancellor Angela Merkel saw Sarkozy's plan as promoting French national interests in the Middle East and in Africa, with the sole intention of establishing a French sphere of influence in the Mediterranean in order to counter Germany's dominant position in central and eastern Europe. Merkel was determined to prevent such a "division of influence" from emerging. Nor was Germany prepared to see German and EU funds used to finance contracts that inevitably would be awarded to French companies.[18] At first, Sarkozy intended to involve only those European states with shorelines bordering the Mediterranean. But following a meeting with the German chancellor in March 2008, he agreed to include all EU member states in the project and to frame the new Union as a natural successor of the

Barcelona Process. Simply put, Merkel succeeded in Europeanizing Sarkozy's Mediterranean vision. As a result, the EU's official policy toward the Euro-Mediterranean region is now the UfM, and all future EMP's initiatives will be implemented through the UfM.

In a follow-up meeting to the July 2008 summit, the Euro-Mediterranean foreign ministers met in Marseilles in November 2008. At the Marseilles meeting they agreed upon an institutional framework and the creation of a secretariat, to be located in Barcelona, to manage the UfM.[19] The meeting also decided that the Arab League would participate in all UfM meetings and that an EU-Arab League Liaison Office, based in Malta, would be created.

The UfM is an inter-governmental international organization composed of 44 members: 27 EU member states and the European Commission; 11 Mediterranean countries, entities[20] and one regional organization: Algeria, Egypt, Israel, Jordan, Lebanon, Mauritania, Monaco, Morocco, the Palestinian Authority, Syria, Tunisia, Turkey and the League of Arab States (the Arab League);[21] and four Adriatic and Balkan countries: Albania, Bosnia-Herzegovina, Croatia and Montenegro.

The new institutional structure of the UfM comprises: biennial meetings of the Euro-Mediterranean heads of state and government; a co-presidency that chairs all UfM meetings and sets the agenda for these meetings; senior officials that are mandated to deal with all aspects of the UfM, a permanent committee based in Brussels and charged with preparing the meetings of the senior officials and ensuring the appropriate follow-up; a secretariat that will be based in Barcelona. It is expected that the UfM secretary general will be Jordanian and there be six deputies assigned from Greece, Israel, Italy, Malta, the Palestinian Authority and Turkey. For Israel this was a significant achievement, the first time that it would hold such a high-level position in any inter-governmental international organization. The UfM secretariat will be responsible for managing the technical aspects of the projects of the UfM, and its activities will be mandated by the ministers of foreign affairs and the senior officials. The secretariat will promote projects in six areas of action that were identified for joint cooperation under the UfM: land and maritime highways, de-pollution of the Mediterranean Sea, energy efficiency, civil security, higher education and research and business development.[22]

Israel and the Union for the Mediterranean

When Sarkozy first raised the idea for a UfM, Israel was ambivalent toward this initiative. Privately Israeli officials were skeptical. Scarred by its experience within the Barcelona Process and the hostility of the Arab world to engaging on cooperative ventures, Israel had little expectation that it would benefit from this new initiative. The centerpiece of its relations with the EU was the European Neighborhood Policy (ENP)[23] and its efforts to develop an upgraded Israeli-EU partnership. Israel, similar to many other Mediterranean ENP countries, sees the ENP, and not the UfM, as where the real content of their relations with Europe are located.[24] However, given Sarkozy's strong support of Israel, Israelis had little choice but to lavish praise on his initiative. An Israeli official privately revealed Israel's approach: "if it was president Jacques Chirac's project, we would have killed this initiative immediately. With Sarkozy it is a different story. The UfM became Sarkozy's obsession and we cannot upset our greatest friend in Europe. We must preserve our good relations with Sarkozy and with France. Israel has no other choice but to openly support the UfM."[25]

Following Sarkozy's victory in the French presidential elections, Israel immediately welcomed the idea of the UfM. Shimon Peres called Sarkozy to congratulate him on his election victory, informing him at the same time "that the idea of a Mediterranean Union was very important" and that he [Shimon Peres] was "interested in discussing it further."[26] In the July 2008 Paris summit for the Mediterranean, Israel gave its wholehearted backing to Sarkozy's initiative. In his speech to the summit prime minister Ehud Olmert enthusiastically declared that he had come to Paris:

> in order to take part in the vision of courageous men. On behalf of the people of Israel, I would like to express our tremendous appreciation for your hard work and your sincere efforts to realize the vision of regional cooperation—a vision of hope, a vision of peace and closeness among the peoples of the Mediterranean. . . . Israel also comes to the table with a large measure of goodwill—the good-will to create partnerships with countries so that there will be economic prosperity and stability in the Middle East . . . Today we must act to create bridges between our nations; today we bear the responsibility for the welfare of our peoples; today we must work together for the Middle East and the entire Mediterranean region—for ourselves, for our children, for the coming generations. Here, in Paris, today, I call, together with you, for the creation of a new economic horizon for the entire region.[27]

Without doubt, the project-based approach of the UfM plays to Israel's strengths. The fields of cooperation outlined in the UfM are areas in which Israel possesses considerable experience and would be able to make a significant contribution. There is also the hope in some Israeli circles that work on the projects in the UfM will facilitate a discreet dialogue with Arab partners on functional areas of mutual concern, thus helping to promote Israel's normalization in the region. Some Israelis even argue that the UfM has the potential to redefine Israel's geostrategic environment and regional identity politics in terms of the Mediterranean instead of the Middle East.[28]

However, as with the Barcelona Process, progress in the UfM and Israel's participation within the UfM projects has become contingent on development within the Israeli-Palestinian conflict. The UfM was one of the immediate victims of the January 2009 war in Gaza. For the past year, the Arab partners have refused to engage with Israel in any of the UfM initiatives and meetings.

The same logic underlying the Arab-Israeli multilateral talks and the Barcelona Process applies equally to the UfM. The Euro-Mediterranean countries can little afford to ignore issues of common concern such as the environment, education, cultural understanding, and so on. At some point these mutual interests will force the partners to cooperate. A true UfM is extremely unlikely, if not impossible, without significant progress being made on resolving the Israeli-Palestinian conflict. Until that point, Israel will look to develop its relations with the EU on a bilateral basis and not within regional cooperative security structures. It is this bilateral dimension that is the focus of the next chapter.

〜

CHAPTER THREE

The Bilateral Nature of Israeli–European Union Relations

"Israel . . . strikes me as the true heart of Europe—a peculiar heart located outside the body."

—Milan Kundera, 1985

Israel was one of the first countries to engage with the European Economic Community (EEC). The first trade agreement between the EEC and Israel dates back to 1964, providing for a partial suspension of common external tariff duties on approximately twenty industrial and commercial products. Six years later, in 1970, a new five-year preferential agreement was signed leading to a staged reduction of Israeli tariffs and in 1975 the first free trade agreement, albeit of a limited scope, was concluded. Israel had been eager to upgrade the 1975 free trade agreement but European leaders had ignored repeated Israeli requests on account of the substantive differences over the peace process with the Palestinians and, in particular, Israel's settlement policies.

The breakthrough between Israel and the PLO with the signing of the Oslo Accords in September 1993 led not only to a marked improvement in the tone of Israeli-European relations but also to a qualitative change in the nature of relations between Israel and the EU. Shortly after the signing of the Oslo Accords, Europe and Israel embarked on negotiations over a new trade agreement. At the Essen summit of heads of state and government, held in December 1994, European leaders gave an impetus to these discussions by deciding that Israel "on account of its high level of economic development" should enjoy *"special status"* in its relations with the EU. The discussions on a new agreement were successfully completed six months later.

The 1995 EU-Israel Association Agreement

On 17 July 1995, the Union's Council of Ministers approved the draft of the EU-Israel Association Agreement (AA) and a final version of this document was signed on 20 November 1995. After a long and politicized ratification process, the Association Agreement finally entered into force on 1 June 2000.[1] The Association Agreement marks a significant upgrade of the 1975 cooperation agreement, which had governed economic ties between Israel and the EC for the previous two decades. It constituted the new legal basis that would govern Israeli-EU relations. The agreement is "mixed" since it was signed by both the European Commission and by all the EU member states. As such, it covers areas where the member states retain treaty-making power and touches on issues which are beyond the competency and authority of the European Commission.[2]

The Association Agreement marks an important milestone in Israeli-European relations. Israeli foreign minister Shimon Peres heralded the agreement as a "further proof of Europe's recognition of its special and preferential relations with Israel." The agreement was seen as having huge political and economic ramifications. The signing of the agreement represented for Israel an important step forward for the development of its economy through its potential integration and the development of closer ties with "one of the three blocs in the new international economic order that has emerged in recent years." Israel was confident that the new agreement—primarily the sections dealing with government procurement, and with research and development—would facilitate increased cooperation between the private sectors of both Israel and the EU, and would decrease Israel's negative balance of trade with the EU.[3]

The signing of the Association Agreement placed Israel in a unique status, making it, in industrial and economic terms, the EMP Mediterranean partner country, aside from Turkey, that has the closest ties to the EU. Israel is the only EMP partner country that reached an industrial standard that is comparable to the countries of the EU, allowing it to cooperate with all EU member states within the terms of the Association Agreement on the basis of full reciprocity.[4] The agreement comprises two elements: (i) a series of economic provisions; and (ii) the institutionalization of a political dialogue between Israel and the EU.

Economically, the agreement expanded significantly the parameters of the free trade area established between Israel and the EC in 1975 and updated the rules of origin making them more flexible. It also granted Israel easier access to public and government procurement markets and simplified trade conditions.[5] Significantly, the agreement forbids the imposition of customs duties on imports and exports between the parties, including customs duties of a fiscal nature. It also facilitated an easing of the terms of trade with regards to procedures. The agreement called for the regulation of the flow of trade in agricultural products in which both sides have a significant interest. For example, in August 2008, within the framework of the Association Agreement, Israel and the EU reached a preliminary agreement on further liberalization of trade concerning agricultural and fishery products.[6]

In addition to the facilitation of general trade, the Association Agreement addressed the possibilities for the phased freedom of movement in financial services and improved cooperation in a number of other areas. The agreement also included a section on the right to establish and supply services and the parties agreed to broaden the scope of the agreement to permit European and Israeli firms to establish themselves in the other's territory and to further liberalize the supply of services by companies to consumers in each other's countries. The agreement specifically refers to financial services and called for cooperation based on agreements for the adoption of common rules and standards for accounting, supervision and regulation of banking, insurance and other financial sectors. In addition, it supported the enhancement of trade in services, called for the abolition of restrictions to capital movements and dealt with the coordination of the social security regimes aiming at easing cross-border movement of workers.[7] However, with the exception of a limited initiative to develop a regional framework protocol for liberalization of trade in services, Israel and the EU have, so far, failed to advance toward achieving closer integration of trade in services as supported by the Association Agreement.[8]

The provisions on economic cooperation concentrated on various sectors where complementarities exist between the Israeli and the European economies or on sectors that promote economic growth and/or employment. Economic cooperation would be attained through regular economic dialogue that encompasses fourteen spheres of economic policy: regional cooperation, industrial cooperation, agriculture, standards, financial services, customs, environment, energy, information infrastructures and telecommunications, tourism, approximation of laws, drugs and money laundering, transportation, and migration.[9] An additional section of the agreement is dedicated to social matters. The Association Agreement called for the creation of an ongoing dialogue in all aspects of mutual interest, and in particular, on questions of unemployment, rehabilitation of disabled people, equal treatment of men and women, labor relations and professional training. The agreement also grants social rights for Israeli workers legally employed in the Union, and for nationals of the EU member states legally employed in Israel.[10] At the request of Israel, it also covered cooperation in new areas such as audiovisual production, cultural and information and communication.[11]

Some of the most significant aspects of the Association Agreement were the provisions aimed at intensifying scientific and technological cooperation. In June 1995, six months before the Association Agreement was signed, the Israeli cabinet had already determined that Israel was interested in signing a Research and Development Agreement with the EU. Israel would press for the *full participation* in the EU's Framework Programs for Research and Technological Development (FP) but would not seek "the right to vote in the committees administrating the various projects."[12] On 31 October 1995 Israel and the EU concluded a Research and Development Agreement through which Israel became the first non-European country to be fully associated with the Union's Framework Programs. Since 1996, Israel has been an active member in successive calls for projects and has become an important source of innovation in both basic and market-oriented research conducted in Europe. The EU is now Israel's second-largest source of research funding, second only to the Israel Science Foundation. As part of the EU's Seventh Research Framework Programme (FP7: 2007–2013) Israel will contribute approximately €440 million as part of its contribution to this program.

The Association Agreement is essentially an economic accord covering all areas of economic and social life. But it is also created as a framework for the institutionalization of a regular political dialogue between Israel and the EU. Prior to the signing of the Association Agreement, there was an occasional exchange of ideas at the ministerial level, often within the framework of gatherings of foreign ministers. But these contacts took place on an ad hoc basis, and were not anchored in any formal agreement. The Association Agreement determined that regular meetings would take place once a year at several working levels, from the most senior ministerial level to senior governmental officials. Israel and the EU agreed to the creation of an Association Council that would meet annually, at the level of foreign ministers, in order to examine major issues arising within the Association Agreement as well as other bilateral or international issues of mutual interest. Any disputes between the parties that the Association Council failed to resolve would be settled by a special arbitration mechanism that was established by the Association Council. The agreement also called for the establishment of an Association Committee, which meets at the official level and consists of representatives of the EU Council, the European Commission and senior Israeli officials. In addition the Association Agreement also created 11 sub-committees at the expert level, for the discussion of professional matters.[13]

The Association Agreement is much more than a free trade agreement, and it has allowed for a continuous dialogue and the emergence of a vast degree of cooperative ventures between Israel and the EU on a range of issues. The agreement established the institutional framework for a dialogue between Israel and the EU but offered little about the political parameters of their relationship. In the preamble, the agreement refers to the traditional links between the EC, its member states and Israel, and the common values that they share. But the agreement failed to articulate what values they actually share or how these values will guide their relations. In Article 2 the parties simply state "their relations, as well as all provisions of the Agreement itself, shall be based on respect for human rights and democratic principles, which guides their internal and international policy and constitutes an essential element of this Agreement." The Association Agreement reveals the lack of any systematic thinking within both Israel and the EU about the nature of Israeli-EU relations beyond the need for closer economic ties. The document is remarkably apolitical. There is a lack of any sense of a grand strategy by either Israel or the EU on ideas that might govern the nature of their future relations. The Association Agreement was a significant economic achievement for Israel. But Israel failed to take the opportunity presented by the discussions on the agreement to articulate any systematic long-term policy toward the EU.[14]

Formally, the Association Agreement is an instrument of the Barcelona Process. The text, however, mentions the Mediterranean only twice in its 154 pages: the first in the title of agreement and the second in a reference to the quality of Mediterranean water and the control and the prevention of marine pollution (Article 50). The text refers only to a broader aim of promoting "regional cooperation with a view to the consolidation of peaceful coexistence and economic and political stability." Rather than truly encouraging Israel to promote economic cooperation with its Mediterranean neighbors, the Association Agreement actually sees Israel's economic place in Europe. The agreement is similar to the "Europe Agreements" that the EU signed in the 1990s with the Central and Eastern European Countries (CEEC) that eventually applied for full EU membership.[15]

The Rules of Origin Dispute, 1997–2004

Since the early 1970s the Arab-Israeli conflict had become a central component in European efforts toward developing common foreign policy. Yet,
the Association Agreement fails to mention the Middle East peace process.
Given the tensions between Israel and Europe over issues such as Jerusalem
and in particular Israel's settlement policy in the West Bank and Gaza during the previous decade, this was a surprising omission. The implementation
of the terms of the Association Agreement was not conditioned by the EU
on the assurance of continued progress in the peace process, and the end of
Israeli occupation of Palestinian territories.

The discussions on drawing up a new economic agreement between Israel
and the EU had gathered pace following the signing of the Oslo Accords.
There was a widespread belief in many policy-making circles that past differences between Israel and Europe over the contours of the resolution of
the Israeli-Palestinian conflict had been overcome and that Israel and the
EU now held similar visions over peace with the Palestinians. These hopes
proved to be short-lived, as was the honeymoon period in Israeli-European
relations. The lack of any conditionality in the Association Agreement
attracted significant criticism, primarily on account of Israel's continuing
policy of expanding and building new settlements in the West Bank and
Gaza. The issue of goods produced in Israeli settlements led to a protracted
dispute between Israel and the EU over the terms of "rules of origin" within
the Association Agreement.

The principle of "rules of origin" is a central element in free trade agreements. Determining the product's country of origin constitutes a critical
component as to whether various customs benefits will be accorded to the
product. The issue of rules of origin is one of the main characteristics in the
1995 Association Agreement between the EU and Israel. The Fourth Protocol of the agreement outlines the rules concerning the origin of products
produced by Israel. The rules also determine a "verification" mechanism of
the origin certificate. This serves as the guiding reference as to whether the
product complies with the requirements of the Association Agreement.

In 1997, the question was raised in various European countries as to
whether the Israeli settlements in the occupied territories (West Bank, Gaza
Strip, East Jerusalem and the Golan Heights) constituted part of the territory
of the State of Israel and whether products produced in those settlements
violated the terms of the rules of origin. Several European customs authorities began to challenge the Israeli customs authority by demanding that it
verify the origin certificates/place of production on goods originating in the

Israeli settlements in the occupied territories. This dispute clouded Israeli-European relations, and it developed into a major source of friction until an agreement was finally reached between Israel and the EU in December 2004. The importance of the rules of origin dispute emerged as the litmus test regarding the legal status of Israeli settlements and the response of the EU to Israeli settlement policies and the illegality of its occupation of Arab land.

Rules of origin define whether a particular product originates in one of the countries party to a free trade agreement, and hence whether the exporter is entitled to tariff concessions granted under the free trade agreement. In other words, rules of origin concern the identification of the "nationality" of a product for customs purposes, and they are the instrument which ensures that tariff concessions granted among parties benefit only products originating in the parties concerned, and not products from other countries or territories.

Rules of origin in EU free trade agreements are typically based on three principles: (i) the definition of the originating products (wholly obtained products or sufficiently processed products); (ii) the use of a proof of origin by the customs authority that issues the origin/movement certificate[16] or by an authorized exporter; and (iii) the administrative cooperation between the parties to the free trade agreement for the approval of the origin certificate and for pre- and post-verification procedures. Above all the rules of origin system is based on mutual trust and on shared responsibilities between the customs authorities of the parties to the free trade agreement. In the case of doubts over the origin of the products to which preference was requested or doubts about the validity of the origin certificate, the importing customs authority returns the certificate to the customs authority of the exporting country for verification procedures and for a confirmation regarding the origin of the products or the validity of the certificate. In such cases, the preference is suspended and securities can be requested in order to safeguard the customs debts. The exporting customs authority has a ten-month period to reply to the importing customs authority. Failure to respond may give rise to a preference decline and to a customs debt. The EU's free trade agreements also provide for a dispute settlement mechanism: discussions at the experts' level, meetings of the Customs Cooperation Committee, discussions at senior officials' and ministerial levels and if no solution is reached, even the intervention of a neutral arbitrator.

Back in 1993, two years prior to the signing of the Association Agreement, the EU had begun to raise questions about the status of Israeli orange juice exported to European markets. The Union suspected that Israeli orange juice producers were mixing Brazilian juice concentrates with Israeli juice, which they then labeled for European markets as "Israeli juices," thereby enjoying the tax preference under EU-Israeli agreements. As the Union was not able to find assurances and concrete evidence of this fraud, the EC published a "First Notice to Importers" informing Community importers that there were grounds for doubt about the validity of the origin certificates for importation of orange juice coming from Israel, and that the importers would be liable for duty recovery. The notice further informed Community import-ers of other problems related to the correct implementation by Israel of the rules of origin regarding the importation of products from Israeli settlements in the occupied territories.[17]

The Fourth Protocol to the 1995 Association Agreement between the EU and Israel defines the concept of "originating products" and the methods of administrative cooperation. The protocol specifies the origin criteria for different categories of products. Products are considered originating in Israel if they are (i) "wholly obtained in Israel"; or (ii) products obtained in Israel which contain materials not wholly obtained in Israel, provided that these materials have undergone sufficient working processing in Israel within the meaning of the Fourth Protocol. The protocol also states the possibility of acquiring originating status. However, the Association Agreement did not allow during the disputed period "diagonal cumulation," that is, export of goods that were substantially manufactured elsewhere were not allowed into the EC, as if they had originated in Israel.[18] Both Israel and the EU agreed that such exports violate the Fourth Protocol on the rules of origin.

Article 83 of the EU-Israel Association Agreement provides that the agreement applies on the one hand to the territories of the Union's member states, and on the other hand "to the territory of the State of Israel." But, significantly, the text does not provide a specific definition as to what con-stitutes the "territory of the State of Israel."

The question of products from Israeli settlements in the occupied ter-ritories was first raised by the European Commission in its July 1997 memo-randum to the Israeli government and again in the Commission's May 1998 communication to the European Council and the European Parliament. In this communication, the Commission concluded that based on all relevant UN General Assembly and Security Council Resolutions, no Israeli settle-ments in the West Bank and Gaza Strip, nor those in East Jerusalem and the Golan Heights could be considered as part of the territory of the State of Israel. In addition, the Commission argued that the EU, through its declara-tions and statements on the conflict, had consistently endorsed the prin-ciples enshrined in all relevant UN General Assembly and Security Council Resolutions. Accordingly, the Commission concluded that the territorial scope of application of the 1995 Association Agreement should be limited to Israel's pre-1967 borders. Thus, exports originating in Israeli settlements in the occupied territories did not qualify for preferential treatment under the terms of the Association Agreement, and any origin certificates issued by Israel for goods produced in Israeli settlements contravened the association's protocol on rules of origin.

The European Commission further argued that Israel's breach of the agreement had placed the Union's member states, as "High Contracting Parties," in violation of Article 1 of the Fourth Geneva Convention.[19] The Commission also maintained that in failing to rectify this situation, it, as the guardian of the Union's treaties, was also in breach of its obligation under EU law. As a result, the Commission recommended that if Israel's "violations of the rules of origin should be confirmed they should be brought to an end."[20] A further two EU fact-finding missions to Israel, in September 1998 and in October 1999, confirmed that Israel was in breach of the provisions concerning the rules of origin.

Israel responded by arguing that under Israeli law, East Jerusalem and the Golan Heights formed part of the territory of the country, and that although the West Bank and Gaza had not been formally annexed to the State of Israel, in practice, however, Israeli jurisdiction applied to all Israeli settlements in these territories.[21] Israel further claimed that the assumption that its territory included the occupied territories had become customary over the years, especially since there had been no official protest from the EU on this subject. Israel tried to reinforce its case by pointing to previous trade agreements between Israel and the EU whereby the occupied territories were regarded as falling under Israeli jurisdiction. In addition, according to the Israeli interpretation of the 1994 Paris Protocol on Economic Relations between Israel and the PLO, the territories of Israel the West Bank and the Gaza Strip constituted a single customs area, implying that all goods from the West Bank and the Gaza Strip should be regarded as originating in Israel.

As a result of the Commission's communication and the findings of the two European missions to Israel, the EU General Affairs and External Relations Council decided in 1998 that the issue should be resolved at the technical level through opening a dialogue on this issue with Israel. Israel reacted angrily to the European position over trade privileges for goods produced in the occupied territories. The director general of the Ministry of Agriculture threatened to cancel the benefits for Palestinian agricultural products under the Paris Agreement and denounced the European move as imposing sanctions on Israel and "defining for us the borders of the State of Israel."[22]

The discussions on finding a solution to this dispute were often long-winded and cumbersome, and Israeli replies frequently failed to provide a satisfactory answer to their European counterparts. The nature of the dispute was transformed from an economic legal issue into a high-profile political dispute. Israeli foot dragging on this issue was testing the limits of European patience. External relations commissioner Chris Patten described the dispute and Israel's responses as becoming tiresome and irritating. In 2001, the Commission decided that it was duty bound to ensure a proper implementation of the Association Agreement and to protect the Union's customs revenues. In November 2001, the Commission decided to clarify its 1997 First Notice to European importers, by publishing a second notice regarding the customs benefits accorded to goods produced in the occupied territories. The second notice warned them that admitting products originating from Israeli settlements with preferential treatment into the Union's markets might give rise to a customs debt.[23]

In July 2003, at the Third Euro-Med trade ministerial meeting, a new protocol was endorsed that allowed for the extension of the Pan-European system of the cumulation of origin to the Mediterranean countries. This would require an amendment to the protocols on the origin of goods in the Association Agreements in order to insert the changes necessary for the application of this diagonal cumulation. Israel strongly supported this initiative, but it was warned that a solution needed to be found to the rules of origin dispute before the Association Agreement could be amended to incorporate this change.[24]

Israel finally succumbed to European pressure on this issue. In December 2004, following a proposal by Ehud Olmert, then Israel's minister for industry, trade and labor, the EU-Israel Customs Cooperation Committee adopted a technical arrangement to the rules of origin dispute which would make a clear distinction between goods produced in Israel and those from Israeli settlements. Under the terms of this "technical arrangement" products from the occupied territories would continue to be labeled as "Made in Israel," but Israel was now also obligated to indicate on all origin certificates the precise location of production of the goods, together with their postcode.[25] In order to assist the Union's customs authorities in the implementation of this arrangement, the Delegation of the European Commission to Israel in cooperation with the EU embassies in Israel prepared a list of Israeli settlements that are considered by the EU to fall beyond Israel's 1967 borders. European representatives were at pains to stress that the agreement was purely a custom measure to enable European customs officials to impose duties in accordance with the Association Agreement, and that it should not be regarded as solution to the differences between Israel and the EU over the geographical applicability of the agreement.

On 1 February 2005, a new notice was issued to customs operators informing them that the EU and Israel had arrived at an agreement for the implementation of the Fourth Protocol of the Association Agreement and that products produced in Israeli settlements beyond the 1967 borders would not be applicable for preferential treatment and that the full rate of customs duty should be applied on the concerned products. The end result of the lengthy dispute allowed Israel to make its point by using "Israel" to describe the location of the settlements, and for the EU not to recognize the legality of Israel's occupation by charging a tariff on goods produced beyond the 1967 borders.

The importance of the rules of origin dispute lies beyond the agreement that was reached between Israel and the EU. The dispute, and its resolution, attracted little attention aside from close observers of Israeli-European relations, but its importance should not be underestimated. The rules of origin dispute was reflective of an important underlying shift in the long-term dynamics of relations between Israel and the EU. For Israel, the agreement was a clear sign of Israel's recognition of the ever-increasing importance of the EU, both economically and politically, and the resultant limits on Israel's power in a globalized, interdependent world. Ehud Olmert justified Israel's climb down and the need to find a solution to this dispute by pointing out that the continued export of all Israeli products (not just those from the settlements) to the 25 countries of the EU had been at stake. Europe's refusal to accept Israel's arguments over the geographical scope of the Association Agreement, and its palpable irritation at Israeli foot dragging on this issue, was a sign of its growing assertiveness and its self-confidence as a player on the Israeli-Palestinian peace process. This was matched by increasingly critical statements by European leaders as to the illegality of Israeli settlements and European criticism over the construction of the separation barrier by Israel.

Israel and the European Neighborhood Policy

In 2004 the EU launched the European Neighborhood Policy (ENP). First proposed in March 2003 as the concept of "wider Europe," the ENP was driven by the EU's internal dynamics resulting from the process of EU enlargement. The adoption of the ENP marked an important shift in the EU's policy toward its southern neighbors. Unlike the Euro-Mediterranean Partnership, the "wider Europe-Neighborhood" policy was not designed to address the socio-economic problems facing the countries on the EU's periphery. Instead the concept of "wider Europe" and ENP envisioned the creation of a ring of countries, each sharing the EU's fundamental values and objectives. These countries would be "drawn into an increasingly close relationship, going beyond co-operation to involve a significant measure of economic and political integration." The prime objective of the ENP was to share the benefits of the EU's enlargement with its neighboring countries in order "to avoid drawing new dividing lines in Europe and to promote stability and prosperity within and beyond the new borders of the Union."[26]

Officially, the "wider Europe-Neighborhood" policy was presented as complementing, and not replacing, the Barcelona Process. In the European Commission's *Strategy Paper on the European Neighborhood Policy*, published in May 2004, the Commission argued that the ENP "would be implemented through the Barcelona Process and the Association Agreements with each partner country." But this was little more than lip service to the Barcelona Process. The adoption of the ENP was a clear departure away from the conception and professed long-term aim of Euro-Mediterranean Partnership, namely the creation of new Euro-Mediterranean region. In 2000, in its five year review of the Barcelona Process, the EU asserted that "multilateralism is now as common as, and even prevalent over, traditional bilateral approaches." Four years later, Europe no longer spoke of an encompassing Euro-Mediterranean region. Now, the regional aspects of the Barcelona Process would serve solely as a complementary role, one that would be limited to the promotion of intraregional trade and sub-regional cooperation in the southern periphery at best.[27]

The ENP abandoned the principle of "regionality" that was inherent in the Barcelona Process, and replaced it with an explicitly "differentiated" and "bilateral" approach. Ties would be developed on a case-by-case basis. The most politically and economically advanced countries, or those most willing to undertake serious political and economic reforms, would be offered the chance to upgrade their ties with the EU. The ENP would offer neighboring countries "the chance to participate in various EU activities, through greater political, security, economic and cultural co-operation" and to give them an eventual stake in the EU's Internal Market. Outlining his vision of future relations with its neighbors, European Commission president Romano Prodi made his famous promise: "sharing everything with the Union but institutions" would be on offer.[28]

Israel warmly welcomed the announcement of the ENP and the opportunities it presented. Speaking before the European Council in July 2003, Israeli foreign minister Silvan Shalom praised the ENP as a "visionary" initiative, and stressed that "[w]e in Israel feel that a new and warmer wind is blowing from the northern shores of the Mediterranean."[29] In particular, Israel was encouraged by the EU's departure from the regional straitjacket of the Euro-Mediterranean Partnership that it so distrusted. Israel now saw a "wiser Europe" that was extending its hand toward building a closer partnership. "Wider Europe" offered Israel the chance of becoming a "nearly European country without renouncing any element of sovereignty." Israel for its part was ready to become a "leading star" in this new initiative.[30]

In a similar vein, EU officials stressed Israel's privileged position within ENP, given its economic and political status. Former enlargement commissioner Günter Verheugen, who was responsible for the emerging policy, declared in front of an Israeli audience in mid-2003:

> I consider Israel to be a natural partner for the EU in the new neighbourhood policy. Although Israel is somewhat untypical of the countries that fall within our neighbourhood . . . our relations will be tailor-made and can range from the status quo to the type of close interconnection that we have with countries like Norway or Iceland in the European Economic Area.[31]

The cornerstone of the ENP are a series of bilateral Action Plans that would address a number of key issue areas ranging from political dialogue and reform, economic ties and trade to questions of energy cooperation, social policy and people-to-people contacts. Each Action Plan would comprise a common set of principles but they would be negotiated with each country in a way that reflected the specificity and the existing state of relations.

Israel responded enthusiastically at the possibility of developing a closer relationship with the EU and immediately opened discussions over drawing up an Action Plan. Negotiations proved to be difficult and nearly broke down a number of times. Israel and Europe came to the table with differing ideas and objectives. The EU was insistent that it received an Israeli commitment affording it a formal role in the peace process, in return for economic concessions. Similarly, Brussels demanded Israel's written acceptance of the principles that would guide the peace process, such as the Roadmap, acceptance of the two-state solution and reference to Weapons of Mass Destruction (WMD). The Israeli negotiators sought to avoid any precise commitment on political issues. Israel's negotiating position relied on the initial "wider Europe" vision as maintained by commissioner Verheugen, implying the upgrading of economic relations with no (or only few) strings attached, whereas the EU had started applying the ENP principle of "positive conditionality" to Israel.

The EU-Israel Action Plan (AP) was finally adopted by the European Commission on 9 December 2004 and endorsed by the EU-Israel Association Council on 13 December 2004.[32] The EU-Israel Action Plan was the first Action Plan to be approved by the European Commission. Its signing was heralded by both Europe and Israel as a significant achievement and an important step in bringing Israel and Europe together. But, given their different starting points, it is not surprising that they focused on different aspects on the Action Plan. EU commissioner for external relations and the neighborhood policy, Benita Ferrero-Waldner, spoke of the importance of the Action Plan and especially its achievement in laying out a common political agenda:

> Israel clearly acknowledges the role of the EU in the Quartet and the need to take into account the viability of a future Palestinian state in counter-terrorist activities. Israel has never been willing to make such commitments in writing to any other partner. The same applies to the commitments Israel has entered into concerning WMD.[33]

Not surprisingly, Israel downplayed the political provisions, and particularly the WMD issue, by stressing that the agreement did not change the parameters of the country's positions. Foreign minister Silvan Shalom welcomed the Action Plan describing it as:

> great progress in relations between Israel and the European Union. . . . The conclusion of the . . . [Action Plan] has brought this relationship to new heights. Israel and the European Union now have a strengthened platform for dialogue and cooperation on enhancing mutual trade and investment, promoting war on terrorism, the fight against anti-Semitism and many other common objectives, including Middle East Peace.[34]

Ron Prossor, the director general of the Israeli foreign ministry, was equally enthusiastic, going so far as to proclaim that Israel had just been offered membership to "a very exclusive club."[35]

The preamble to the Action Plan speaks of the opportunity afforded by enlargement for "the EU and Israel to develop an increasingly close relationship, going beyond co-operation, to involve a significant measure of economic integration and a deepening of political co-operation." Although the Action Plan is based on the 1995 Association Agreement it lays out a much wider and more comprehensive set of jointly developed Israeli-EU priorities, and opens up the possibility for Israel to participate progressively in key aspects of EU policies and programs.

The Action Plan identifies six key areas of cooperation and joint action between Israel and Europe. It places a special emphasis on the "upgrade in the scope of political cooperation" by calling for a renewed political dialogue "based on shared values, including issues such as the promotion and the protection of human rights and fundamental freedoms; improving the dialogue between cultures and religions; promoting effective multilateralism in the framework of the UN; combating anti-Semitism, racism, xenophobia and Islamophobia."[36] The Action Plan also calls for an enhanced dialogue on efforts to resolve the Middle East conflict; containing the spread of WMD and their means of delivery including ballistic missiles; the question of the illicit trafficking of military equipment; and strengthening the fight against terrorism. In the economic sphere, the Action Plan speaks of increasing economic integration by developing trade and investment flows, by liberalizing trade and services, in particular financial services with a view to prepare Israel for participation in the EU market, as well as deepening and enhancing the existing economic dialogue and identifying areas relevant for regulatory approximation with EU legislation. The Action Plan also details a range of programs and common initiatives which cover the following four issue areas: (i) strengthening cooperation on migration related issues, fight against organized crime, including trafficking in human beings and police and judicial cooperation; (ii) promoting cooperation in science and technology, research and development, the information society, transport, energy and telecom networks; (iii) strengthening the environmental dimension of public policy; and (iv) strengthening links and cooperation in "people-to-people" contacts in education, culture, civil society and public health.

Since its adoption five years ago, the Action Plan has enabled Israel and Europe to intensify the level of their dialogue in the field of political and security cooperation, raise significantly the degree of economic integration and has helped boost socio-cultural and scientific cooperation. Institutional cooperation through the EU-Israel Association Council, the EU-Israel Association Committee and 11 sub-committees have brought together EU and Israeli experts to oversee the implementation of the Action Plan. In period 2007–2010, Israel has received €2 million annually in EU assistance to help support activities aimed at implementing the priority areas outlined in the Action Plan. Several Israeli ministries already have adopted ENP Action Plan implementation programs, while other ministries are in the midst of developing such programs.

Five years into the implementation phase of the Action Plan, Israel has been actively exploiting the possibilities offered by ENP to participate in EU programs. For example, in November 2007 Israel was the first ENP partner country to join the Competitiveness and Innovation Framework Program (CIP) under which the EU promotes innovation, entrepreneurship and growth of small and medium-sized enterprises (SMEs).[37] Negotiations aimed at achieving a greater Israeli-EU reciprocal liberalization of trade in agricultural, processed agricultural products and fish and fishery products were concluded in April 2008. In the transport field, the EC and Israel have signed a horizontal aviation agreement and started negotiations over a comprehensive aviation agreement. Israel and the EU also signed a joint declaration on cooperation and dialogue in education and training. The protocol on the general principles governing Israel's participation in Community programs was also signed in April 2008.[38]

Without question, the adoption of the Action Plan marks an important turning point in Israeli-European relations. Its provisions are reflective of the scope and growing importance of Europe to the Israeli economy. It was also negotiated during a turbulent period in Israeli-European relations. Addressing the European Council of Ministers in July 2003, Israeli foreign minister Silvan Shalom spoke of the "common values and interests that make us natural partners in the quest for peace in the Middle East. Israel respects the wish of Europe to play a role, and we acknowledge the contribution of the EU both to the Palestinian economy and to the U.S.-led effort of shaping the performance-based Roadmap."[39] His comments masked over the various differences between Israel and Europe and the increasingly bitter exchanges during those years. Exactly one year after Shalom's speech in Brussels, Israeli-European relations reached a new low. All twenty-five member states of EU, in spite of intensive lobbying by Israel, supported a UN General Assembly Resolution condemning Israel for its construction of the separation wall/fence in the West Bank, and demanding its immediate dismantlement. In response, the Israeli Ministry of Foreign Affairs launched a withering attack on the EU, castigating its leaders for their willingness to blindly support Palestinian positions at the cost of the security of Israeli citizens, and that through its action the EU was only encouraging the Palestinian leadership to forego its responsibility in fighting terror.[40]

But at the same time, Israel was beginning to acknowledge the importance of the EU as an emerging political actor that it could no longer brush aside. The resolution of the rules of origin dispute was an indication that Israel could no longer simply ignore European positions on the Israeli-Palestinian conflict. At heart, the Action Plan can be viewed as a wish list of potential future areas of economic cooperation between Israel and the EU.[41] However, the Action Plan attempts to broaden the dialogue between Israel and the EU beyond the economic sphere and the immediacy of the Arab-Israeli conflict.

The document makes reference to a number of political issues and highlights several common areas of future cooperation such as the fight against terrorism, the protection of human rights, and the non-proliferation of WMDs. The language used to cover those issues is deliberately vague, ignoring fundamental differences between the EU and Israel. The Action Plan also lacks political commitment. The commitments made by Israel are, at best, ambiguous and leaving them open to future misunderstandings and conflicting interpretations by both sides.[42]

The Action Plan's section on "shared values" commits the two parties to the promotion of "the shared values of democracy, rule of law . . . respect for human rights . . . international humanitarian law . . . the rights of minorities . . . evaluation and monitoring of policies from the perspective of gender equality." But the document does not talk of any joint programs or of creating any benchmarks for the protection of human rights. Instead, it refers meekly to exploring *"the possibility"* (our italics) to join the optional protocols related to international conventions on human rights," without detailing which conventions. A similar observation can be made concerning the question of the protection of minorities. Israel's 2003 amendment to the law on Israeli citizenship drew considerable criticism from international as well as Israeli human rights organizations. The EU's Country Report on Israel, which served as the basis for the Action Plan, strongly criticized Israel for the amended law. Yet the Action Plan is conspicuously silent on this issue.[43] The Action Plan does not suggest any mechanisms for developing an Israeli-EU dialogue on the question of human rights and the protection of Israel's Palestinian citizens. All that is left are bland European comments on the lack of progress in this area. The 2008 *Progress Report on the Implementation of the European Neighbourhood Policy* simply states, "progress with regard to the promotion of democracy, rule of law and respect for human rights and international humanitarian law was limited. . . . Overall, the promotion and protection of the Israeli Arab minority remained unsatisfactory during the reporting period."[44]

The language, however, is much more direct when the Action Plan discusses the fight against anti-Semitism. It explicitly refers to the Berlin declaration of the Organization for Security and Co-operation in Europe (OSCE) conference on anti-Semitism of April 2004 and commits both sides to work for the speedy implementations of its conclusions. The Action Plan also details a number of specific measures, such as the strengthening of the legal framework, the promotion of education about the Holocaust, the support for civil society and international organizations in their efforts to combat anti-Semitism, and the exchange of information among experts on best practices.

Combating anti-Semitism was high on the Israeli agenda and as a result the Action Plan includes several references to anti-Semitism, even though the EU usually refers to this issue as part of its broader fight against racism and xenophobia. The inclusion of the fight against anti-Semitism in the Action Plan came under attack by some European Jewish community leaders and several prominent European Jewish scholars. They saw anti-Semitism as an issue to be addressed by their own communities and not by Israel. They were also critical of the inclusion of the clauses on the protection of minority languages, mainly Yiddish and Ladino.[45] For them, these two languages belong to the European Jewish communities and have nothing to do with the two official languages of the State of Israel: Hebrew and Arabic, or any of the official languages of any EU member state.[46]

The most problematic issue in the Action Plan surrounds the surprising inclusion of WMDs as one of the issues for future dialogue. The Action Plan states that Israel and the EU will "cooperate on non-proliferation of weapons of mass destruction, and their means of delivery including ballistic missiles, including through implementing UNSC resolution 1540/04 . . . and consider the promotion of adherence, implementation, accession and strengthening of other relevant international instruments." This dialogue will be based on two documents: the first entitled "EU Strategy against Proliferation of Weapons of Mass Destruction" from December 2003, which commits the EU to promote a non-proliferation policy in its external relations; and the second document, "Israel's Vision on the Long-Term Goals of Regional Security and Arms Control Process in the Middle East." Israel was almost excluded from the ENP due to its refusal to include the provisions on non-proliferation of WMD in the Action Plan. It was only after the EU warned Israel that the Action Plan might not be adopted was it willing to compromise on this issue. It still required an additional six weeks of negotiations over the exact wording of the WMD section.[47]

Given Israel's refusal to discuss its non-conventional capabilities, the EU portrayed the inclusion of the WMD as a significant achievement. Not surprisingly Israel downplayed this issue, noting that in the 1995 Barcelona declaration it had previously agreed to work on "preventing the proliferation of nuclear, chemical and biological weapons through adherence to and compliance with international and regional non-proliferation regimes and the various arms control and disarmament agreements."[48] More significantly, Israel and the EU have not engaged in any meaningful dialogue on this issue since the adoption of the Action Plan five years ago.

From Special Status to Upgrade

Shortly before taking over the EU Presidency in January 2007, Israel convinced the German government that it should revisit the 1994 Essen declaration during its term in office. At the heads of state meeting in Essen in December 1994, the EU had determined that Israel should "enjoy special status in its relations with the European Union on the basis of reciprocity and common interest." But since the issuing of that statement, neither Israel nor Europe had given much thought to what this "special status" might mean in practice. The Essen declaration had marked a high point in Israeli-European relations, coming in the aftermath of the Oslo Accords and the signing of the peace treaty between Israel and Jordan. But this rapprochement between Israel and Europe was short-lived. The decade following Essen was marked by sharp disagreements between Israel and Europe over the peace process with the Palestinians. As discussed in chapter 1, those disagreements had often been accompanied by bitter exchanges between Israel and the EU.

The desire for a formal upgrade of its relations with the EU was reflective of a steady shift in Israeli thinking about the growing importance of Europe for its economic development, and the potential role the EU might play in guaranteeing Israel's overall security. Seven years of fighting Palestinian insurgency, the seemingly endless cycle of action and reaction, the degeneration of the Palestinian political environment and the failure of its military campaign in Lebanon in the summer of 2006 had led to a rethinking in Israeli policy circles as to the utility of military force to meet the security challenges it faced. This was accompanied by a growing receptiveness in Israel to engage with the EU on how to meet those challenges. Differences still remained with the EU about the peace process. But there had also been a steady convergence in Israeli and European thinking over the strategies needed to bring the Israeli-Palestinian conflict to an end.

The idea of developing closer ties with the EU had been gaining support from members of the political establishment and, as will be discussed in chapter 4, from large sectors of the Israeli public. Most significantly, promoters of closer relations with the EU had found a new champion in Tzipi Livni, who had been appointed in May 2006 as Israel's foreign minister. In a speech to a conference on Israeli-EU relations in December 2006, Livni outlined her vision of future relations: "I truly believe that the road should ultimately lead us to a significant participation of Israel in the European integration project. And here the sky is the limit."[49]

The EU responded positively to Israel's request. On 5 March 2007 a "Reflection Group," comprising the Israeli government, the European Commission and the Council Secretariat, was established, charged with the task of examining areas in which cooperation between Israel and the EU could be enhanced. Based on its preliminary findings, the EU-Israel Association Council convened in Luxembourg on 16 June 2008, and agreed to intensify Israeli-EU relations within the framework of the ENP. The upgrade of relations would be carried out in three areas:

1. Increased diplomatic cooperation—there would be an institutionalization of the diplomatic dialogue, by means of regular annual meetings at a senior level. In addition, the Luxembourg statement called for an increase in the number of meetings between government ministers, senior officials and parliamentarians from both sides;
2. Israeli participation in European agencies, working groups and programs—with a view to achieving greater convergence toward the EU *acquis communautaire*. This will bring the Israeli society and economy closer to European norms and standards and will increase the competitiveness of Israeli companies in the European market. It will also lead to the recognition by European academic institutions of degrees awarded by Israeli universities and colleges;
3. Israel's integration into the European Single Market—a joint working group would examine the areas in which Israel possesses the capacity of integrating into the European Single Market. This would lay the groundwork for the further upgrading of Israeli-EU relations in the future.

In order to implement this decision, the EU and Israel started to review the content of the Action Plan. Meetings of all joint subcommittees were tasked with producing specific proposals that would guide Israeli-EU relations past April 2009. Unlike the 1995 Association Agreement and the initial Action Plan, the EU now conditioned the process of upgrading relations with Israel on progress in the peace process with the Palestinians. In the Luxembourg statement, the EU emphasized its commitment to develop a closer relationship with Israel but that "such a partnership will imply a stronger involvement of the European Union in the peace process and in the monitoring of the situation on the ground." It added that "the process of developing a closer EU-Israeli partnership *needs to be, and to be seen* (our italics), in the context of the broad range of our common interests and objectives which notably include the resolution of the Israeli-Palestinian conflict through the implementation of the two-state solution."[50]

In December 2008, the EU reaffirmed in Brussels its determination to upgrade bilateral relations and issued guidelines for strengthening the political dialogue structures with Israel. The Brussels guidelines call for the following: convening ad hoc summits at the level of heads of state and government as well as three meetings a year at the foreign minister level; allowing for each EU Presidency to invite, on an ad hoc basis, the director general of Israel's Ministry of Foreign Affairs to one of the meetings held during its term of office; providing for hearings of Israeli experts by Council working parties and committees; organizing systematic and broader informal strategic consultations; intensifying exchanges on human rights and anti-Semitism; encouraging Israel to remain in line with Common Foreign and Security Policy (CFSP) positions; enabling cooperation in the context of the European Security and Defense Policy (ESDP); encouraging Israeli integration and involvement in multilateral fora; and intensifying inter-parliamentary dialogue.[51]

Two weeks after the Brussels meeting, Israel launched Operation Cast Lead in response to the breakdown of the cease-fire between Israel and Hamas and the launching of missiles attacks from Gaza on Israeli cities in the south of the country. European leaders were outspoken in their criticism of Israel's 22-day military (re)invasion of Gaza which left over 1,400 Palestinians dead, and of Israel's subsequent economic blockade of Gaza. The EU led calls for the lifting of Israel's siege. "Gazans have the right to clean drinking water, electricity and food," European commissioner for external relations Benita Ferrero-Waldner told Israel. She added, "Israel has an obligation to ensure Palestinians can assert these rights. Immediate, unconditional, sustained and predictable opening of the crossings to and from Gaza is essential." Tensions between Israel and the EU were also exacerbated over the refusal of the new Likud-led government in Israel to support the creation of a Palestinian state. Ferrero-Waldner reminded Israel that the EU "as Israel's partner and friend, expects the new Israeli government to help implement the vision of a two-state solution. Recent activities intended to create new facts on the ground in and around Jerusalem run counter to this vision. Living up to past agreements, including those made in the context of multilateral forums, is essential."[52]

In response to these new Israeli-EU tensions, discussions over upgrading relations were put on hold by the Union. None of the Israel-EU sub-committees mandated to discuss the content of the upgrade were convened. Plans by the Czech government to hold an EU-Israel summit during its 2009 EU Presidency to mark the upgrading of relations were quietly shelved. In April 2009, Ferrero-Waldner told reporters that Israel must support the creation of a Palestinian state and recommit to the Middle East peace process before the EU could consider deepening its ties, and that, to her mind, the time was not ripe to move beyond the current level of relations. Her remarks brought a harsh rebuke from the new Israeli government, but also led to a plea from Tzipi Livni, now leader of the opposition, for the EU not to suspend discussions over the upgrading of relations.[53] Although the EU has refrained from formally suspending the upgrade, in effect the process has been frozen. At the meeting of the EU-Israel Association Council, held in Luxembourg in June 2009, the EU restated that the process needed to be seen in the broader context of sustained progress toward a resolution of the Israeli-Palestinian conflict, and that "at this stage the EU proposes that the current Action Plan remain the reference document for our relations until the new instrument is adopted."[54]

Talk of upgrading ties has been effectively frozen and is unlikely to resume until significant progress is made toward the establishment of a Palestinian state. Upgrading Israel's formal standing is unlikely to feature as a high priority on the EU's agenda in the near future. Until that time, Israel and the EU need to debate the institutional arrangements that might govern their future relations. This is a theme that we will address in chapter 5.

~

CHAPTER FOUR

Israeli (Mis)Perceptions
of the European Union

"We are absolutely European in all our feelings and thoughts."

—Marcus Ehrenpreis (a leading Zionist thinker), 1897

Europe is Israel's economic, cultural and, in many respects, political hinterland. Israel enjoys a unique status in its relations with the EU, a status that grants it extensive rights in many areas such as research and development and economics. The importance of Europe to Israel was recognized by Israel's foreign minister Tzipi Livni. In one of her more important statements on Europe, Livni expressed her belief in the potential of Israeli-European relations: "I truly believe that the road should ultimately lead us to a significant participation of Israel in the European integration project. And here the sky is the limit."[1] Livni's comments are reflective of a changing attitude within Israeli policy-making circles and civil society toward the EU. Yet over the years, Europe has not always been central to Israeli strategy and has rarely been seen in a positive light. These negative images and perceptions have led to Israel behaving more as if it were an island in the Atlantic Ocean than a Mediterranean country neighboring the European continent.

This chapter is based on a study conducted under the *Network of Excellence Global Governance, Regionalisation and Regulation: The Role of the EU*—GARNET, and an earlier version of it was published in Sonia Lucarelli and Lorenzo Fioramonti, eds., *External Perception of the European Union as a Global Actor* (Oxon and New York: Routledge, 2009), 70–86.

This chapter explores the changing images and perceptions in Israel of the EU among the general public, political elites, organized civil society and the Israeli press. An evaluation of the perceptions held by Israelis—and in some cases only by dispelling them—will allow for a better understanding of the challenges Israel and Europe have to overcome to put Israeli-European relations on a more stable footing. A similar study of European images and perceptions of Israel needs to be undertaken, but that is beyond the scope of this chapter. This survey was carried out through interviewing Israeli politicians and policy makers; leaders, directors and board members of Israel's leading trade unions, academic institutions and non-governmental organizations (NGOs); and leading journalists of major Israeli newspapers, television channels and radio programs. In analyzing Israel's civil society, we conducted a survey of 100 websites of major Israeli trade unions, academic institutions and NGOs. The Internet search was based on a search for the terms "European Union" and "Europe." We also carried out a content analysis of the three leading national Hebrew newspapers, *Haaretz*, *Yedioth Ahronoth* and *Maariv*, between 1 October 2007 and 31 March 2008.

The chapter reveals that Israelis hold three contradictory views about the EU. First, that many Israelis see the Union as a hospitable framework for Israeli accession, and consequently believe Israel should explore joining the EU in the near future. At the same time, they do not see close political relations with the EU as essential for Israel. Finally, that anti-Israeli attitudes and geo-strategic views detrimental to the security of Israel are deeply embedded within the EU. Underlying this perception is the widespread view that anti-Semitism remains a serious problem in many of the member states of the EU.

The European Union as a Global Power

In the course of this study we distributed a questionnaire on the dominant powers of the 21st century and on the nature of international politics. The interviewees include Israeli politicians and policy makers; leaders, directors and board members of Israel's leading trade unions, academic institutions and NGOs; and leading journalists of major Israeli newspapers, television channels and radio programs. The results of this questionnaire are summarized in table 4.1.[2]

The interviewees place both the EU and France together in fourth place on the list of global superpowers after the U.S., China, Russia and Germany—but they also expect the EU to move up to third place by the year 2020. According to our interviewees, among the greatest challenges facing the

Table 4.1.   Results of a Questionnaire on the Dominant Powers of the 21st Century and the Nature of International Politics, 40 Israeli Interviewees (Jan.–May 2008)

Statement / Opinion	Percentage Points / Challenges / Goals
The EU is a superpower already today	33%
The EU will be a superpower in 2020	50%
The biggest challenges to the world's superpowers	1. Climate change
	2. International terrorism
	3. Poverty
The top goals of any superpower	1. Protection of the environment
	2. Peace keeping
	3. Non-proliferation of WMDs
The EU is the best framework to maintain peace and stability in the world	33%
A unipolar international system might have a positive effect on the maintenance of world peace	17%

Source: Pardo, Eskenazi and Kantz (2008).

world's superpowers are climate change, international terrorism, and poverty. Consequently, protection of the environment, peace-keeping, and the eradication of poverty should be the top goals of any superpower.

About 50 percent of our interviewees were of the opinion that the U.S. is the country best placed to maintain peace and stability in the world, while 33 percent were of the opinion that it is the EU, rather than the U.S., which is best placed for assuring world peace. Only 17 percent of the interviewees thought that a unipolar international system might have a positive effect on the maintenance of world peace, while 33 percent were of the opinion that world peace could be maintained under EU leadership or under balanced regional superpowers.

The European Union's Involvement in the Middle East Peace Process

In spite of the adoption of the successful bilateral instruments and the recent decision for an upgrading of Israeli-EU relations, political relations between Israel and the EU have never fully recovered from the heavy shadow cast by the 1980 Venice declaration. From that point on, the EU has been seen by Israel as harboring a strong pro-Arab bias and an antipathy to Israel and its security. The positions adopted by the EU on the Arab-Israeli conflict have been seen in Israel as hostile to Israeli policies and concerns. Indeed, the EU and all its member states have been vocal in their criticism of Israeli policies over the past three decades. The harsh tone of much of this criticism has drowned out their expressed commitment to the existence and survival of Israel. Without question, European declarations and speeches have strongly shaped Israeli attitudes toward the EU, especially in respect to a potential role for the EU in the Middle East peace process.

Unsurprisingly the survey confirmed the view that Israelis do not see the EU as a significant player in the Middle East peace process. In the Konrad-Adenauer-Stiftung (KAS) and Pardo 2007 national survey on Israelis' attitudes toward the EU and its member states, 75 percent of the Israeli public believed that either the U.S. or EU member states should be involved in the peace process between Israel and its neighbors. When the respondents to the KAS and Pardo 2009 national survey were asked the same question, 56 percent of the respondents replied the U.S. as opposed to 9 percent who said they preferred the EU. In addition, 34 percent of the respondents to the 2009 survey felt that EU involvement in the region in recent years prevented progress in the peace process.[3]

At the same time, it is important to note that Israelis understand that the Union's policies toward the Israeli-Palestinian conflict are reflective of the EU's increasing importance as an actor on the global stage. The EU involvement in reaching a cease-fire in the Gaza Strip in January 2009, the EU Border Assistance Mission (EUBAM) in Rafah, and member states' military involvement in the UN Interim Force (UNIFIL II) in southern Lebanon are testimonies to the Union's increased involvement in the Middle East in the field of security. These missions, and their acceptance by Israel, mark a significant step forward for Israeli-European relations, insofar as they established a precedent whereby the EU has been afforded a responsibility in the "hard security" sphere.

Israeli Perceptions of the EU: Public Opinion and Political Elites

Public Opinion

Israeli perceptions are often analyzed as if Israel were a single, coherent, unified society. This is clearly not the case. Various sectors of Israeli society hold differing views on the EU, and differences exist within each sector as well. Nevertheless, it is possible to identify certain perceptions that are widely shared by both the general public and by political elites.

There is a widespread perception among Israelis that the EU represents a hospitable framework for Israeli accession, and therefore that Israel should

Table 4.2. Importance Attributed to Israel Joining the EU

	Entire sample	Jews	Immigrants	Arabs
Very important	44	44	27	43
Important	26	25	45	34
Somewhat important	14	15	16	10
Not very important	9	10	9	5
Not important	2	2	2	5
Not important at all	4	4	1	3
Don't Know	1	—	—	—
Total	100%	100%	100%	100%

Source: Dahaf (2004).

seek membership of the EU within the foreseeable future. This perception is driven by Israelis' hopes, desires and by their expectation of the possibility of joining the Union.

In a Dahaf 2004 survey of Israelis' perceptions of the EU, 70 percent of those surveyed thought that joining the EU was either very important or important (see table 4.2).[4] In the KAS and Pardo 2009 national survey, an overwhelming majority, 69 percent, of the Israeli public either "strongly supported" or "somewhat supported" the idea that Israel should join the EU (see table 4.3.). In addition, following the EU enlargement in January 2007, about 40 percent of the Israelis were identified as eligible for EU citizenship.[5]

An additional perception, seemingly contradictory to the first perception, is that strong political relations with the EU are not that essential for Israel. In the Dahaf 2004 survey of Israeli public opinion, more than two-thirds (68 percent) of people polled considered relations with the U.S. as more important than relations with the EU. Furthermore, only 6 percent considered relations with the EU as more important than relations with the U.S.

Table 4.3. Degree of Support for Israel Joining the EU

	Entire sample	Jews	Arabs	Immigrants
Strongly Support	42	45	24	48
Somewhat Support	27	31	15	29
Somewhat Oppose	9	9	11	11
Strongly Oppose	9	7	19	6
Don't Know/ Refused	13	8	31	6
Total	100%	100%	100%	100%

Source: KAS and Pardo (2009).

About one quarter (26 percent) thought that both relations are equally important.[6] Furthermore, 69 percent of the respondents to the KAS and Pardo 2007 survey said that in thinking about Israeli culture, they felt that Israel shared more in common with America than with Europe. Only 20 percent of the respondents felt they held more in common with Europeans than with Americans.[7]

The third perception follows from the second and accentuates the tension with the first, namely, that anti-Israeli attitudes and geo-strategic views detrimental to the security of Israel are embedded in the EU. Underlying this perception is a common belief among Israelis that anti-Semitism is prevalent in large parts of the EU.

The 2007 KAS and Pardo survey reveals that 78 percent of those surveyed held that the EU is not doing enough to counter anti-Semitism in Europe.[8] Likewise 64 percent of the respondents to the Dahaf 2004 survey agreed with the claim that the EU positions toward Israel are reflective of anti-Semitic attitudes thinly disguised as moral principles.[9]

Political Elites

A number of Israeli politicians share the public's position that Israel is in a position to, and should, seek EU membership in the near future. For instance, a group of Israeli parliamentarians representing a broad spectrum of Israel's political parties signed a manifesto in 2002 advocating Israeli membership in the EU.[10] In November 2002, then foreign minister Binyamin Netanyahu, declared that Israel favored joining the EU and asked Italy to help Israel achieve this goal.[11] Likewise, former foreign minister and current vice prime minister Silvan Shalom stated in May 2003 that the Israeli government was weighing the possibility of applying for EU membership, adding that "we will be glad to be accepted by the EU."[12] In January 2007, Avigdor Liberman, then minister of strategic affairs and currently deputy prime minister and minister of foreign affairs, declared that "Israel's diplomatic and security goal . . . must be clear: joining NATO and entering the EU."[13] Likewise, Liberman's party's (Yisrael Beytenu) platform ahead of the February 2009 general elections stated that:

> One of the clear goals of Yisrael Beytenu is Israel's joining the European Union and NATO. To date, most of Israel's trade is with the European Union, and hundreds of thousands of Israelis hold dual European citizenships. Additionally there is a strong cultural bond between Israel and Europe; it is hard to imagine modern Europe without the influence of Jewish intellectuals, from Spinoza to Kafka and Freud. Membership in the European Union would gain Israel greater

political influence in an ever-strengthening Europe and contribute much to the economy. We can achieve this goal in the near future and should make every effort to make it come about.[14]

A different approach has been taken by Israel's President, Shimon Peres, who has argued that once Israel, the Palestinians and Jordan sign a peace agreement, "they should be accepted as members of a united Europe," in which the three countries could form a trading partnership creating "a modern Benelux." According to Peres, offering membership of the EU "will give hope to the three parties."[15]

Importantly, there are also voices in the EU that support such thinking, feeding this Israeli perception that Israeli membership in the EU is possible. For example, Italian prime minister Silvio Berlusconi has for several years, and especially during the 2003 Italian Presidency of the EU, been advocating Israel's accession to the EU. In 2004, Berlusconi declared that "Italy will support Israeli membership in the EU. . . . As far as Italy is concerned, Israel is completely European in terms of standard of living, heritage and cultural values. Geography is not a determinant."[16] More recently, in his January 2009 visit to Jerusalem, Berlusconi reiterated his earlier statements, announcing that "despite the geographic distance, one day Israel can be one of the member countries in the European Union. I am still convinced that it is proper that this happen, and we must continue working to that end."[17]

Israel is also considered to be a natural candidate for EU membership by French president Nicolas Sarkozy—or at least a more natural partner than Turkey. In his 2007 election campaign manifesto Sarkozy explained: "if Turkey entered the EU, I also wonder on what basis we could exclude Israel, so many of whose citizens are at home in France and in Europe, and vice versa."[18] Support for Israeli accession to the EU can also be heard in the European Parliament. The Transnational Radical Party, for instance, has for many years been running a campaign for full Israeli membership in the EU.[19] Also according to the former junior partner in Germany's coalition government, the Social Democrats (SPD), Israel could join the EU. The party's foreign affairs spokesman, Gert Weisskirchen, recently told the *Hamburger Abendblatt* daily that "I really wish Israel becomes a full member of the European Union. Israeli membership is something that can be considered in 15 years."[20]

Although Israeli policy makers are aware of the importance of the EU to Israel, like the general public, many of them share the public's view that good political relations with the EU are not crucial for Israel. In a statement that well reflects Israeli disregard of European opinion, former prime minister,

Ariel Sharon, told a gathering of Israeli ambassadors to Europe that they should pay no heed to criticism of Israel by European governments since Israel "does not owe anyone [i.e., the Europeans] anything. We are obligated only to God!"[21] Echoing the same attitude, in January 2009 former prime minister Ehud Olmert defended Israel's incursion of the Gaza Strip by dismissing European criticisms:

> We wanted the people in southern Israel to be able to sleep. . . . Is this exaggerated? Is this not what every country would do for its citizens? I heard all kinds of moral preaching from [European] states. And I ask, after all this nation has been through, who has the right to say that we do not have the right to defend this nation?[22]

Only three weeks after his return to power, Israeli prime minister Binyamin Netanyahu took a similar approach toward Europe. In dismissing European calls to suspend the upgrade of Israeli-European relations, Netanyahu told the Czech premier, Mirek Topolanek, that Europe "should not set conditions for us."[23]

Israeli political elites also share the public's perception that EU policies toward Israel are colored by anti-Semitism. In the last eight years, European anti-Semitism was discussed several times by the Israeli government in its weekly meetings. In press statements issued by Israeli politicians following meetings with European officials, the topic of European anti-Semitism is regularly cited.

In November 2003 in an interview to *EUpolitix.com*, Ariel Sharon said "an ever stronger Muslim presence in Europe is certainly endangering the life of the Jewish people . . . I would say . . . EU governments are not doing enough to tackle anti-Semitism. . . . Of course it is dangerous to generalize, but it is possible to say that the majority of countries in Europe do not have a balanced policy towards Israel."[24] The following year he warned the Israeli Knesset that "the anti-Semitism virus woke again in Europe and is beginning to infect large parts of the continent."[25] In mid-2004, he told a meeting of the American Jewish Association in Jerusalem that Jews around the world should relocate to Israel as early as possible. For Sharon, Jews living in France were in particular danger, and moving to Israel for them was a "must" because of the rise of anti-Semitism in France and in Europe. In Sharon's words: "we see the spread of the wildest [European] anti-Semitism."[26] Former foreign minister Tzipi Livni, although a strong advocate of Israeli-European relations, has painted a bleak picture: "anti-Semitism is still very much alive [in Europe]. . . . As the home of all the Jewish people, this is a fight that should be led by Israel," Livni told participants of the foreign ministry's Global Forum for

Combating Anti-Semitism. According to Livni, "modern anti-Semitism is spreading from fringes to the mainstream, in parallel with the growth of radical Islamic ideology in Europe. It poses a significant threat. We are witnessing new types of cooperation in Europe between the racist right, radical left and the Jihadist Muslims in this campaign."[27]

The fight against anti-Semitism in Europe is also included in the EU-Israel Action Plan as well as in the December 2008 EU Council guidelines for strengthening the political dialogue structures with Israel. Several chapters and sections of the Action Plan include references to anti-Semitism; the section on "shared values" contains a special subsection on "combating anti-Semitism" in which both parties commit themselves to the struggle against all forms of anti-Semitism in Europe. In the December 2008 Council guidelines, the EU and Israel also agreed to replace their informal working group on human rights by a formal subcommittee on human rights, which is to examine, among other matters, the "fight against racism and xenophobia—including Islamophobia and anti-Semitism."[28]

Analysis of Public Opinion and Political Elites' Perceptions of the EU[29]

The general public's perception that the EU represents a hospitable framework for Israeli accession, and therefore that Israel is ready and should join the EU within the foreseeable future is easy to understand. Such a perception can be best explained by Israeli wishful thinking. What is more surprising is the degree to which senior Israeli officials as well as European leaders, policy-makers and others who are familiar with the workings of the EU cling to this idea. Proponents of Israeli membership of the EU ignore fundamental incongruities between Israel's self-definition as a Jewish state and the state of the Jewish people, on the one hand, and the guiding principle of the EU of an open and unified space without sharp distinctions between citizens of member states in terms of "insiders" and "others." Israel is a liberal democratic state, but Israel's self-definition as a Jewish state and the state of the Jewish people makes it exceptional and radically different from other states. There is a clear contradiction between the Israeli Law of Return[30] and the EU principle of freedom of movement of persons, even if realized in phases. Further factors include ethnocentric criteria in Israeli educational and socio-economic policies and overall policies of Israel with regard to promoting the welfare of the Jewish people. Such tendencies and policies are not in line with broader EU values.

This fundamental difference would present significant obstacles for Israeli accession to the EU, even if Israel were invited by Europe to apply for membership. This core value would be difficult, if not impossible, for Israel relinquish, since for many Israelis this difference underscores the entire *raison d'être* for the existence of Israel as an independent state.

Israel is not regarded by EU institutions and officials as a likely candidate for joining the Union in the foreseeable future. Commissioner Benita Ferrero-Waldner explained: "in the context of the [ENP] we still have a lot of work to bring Israel and the EU closer . . . as for the question of [Israel's] EU membership—this question is not on the agenda."[31] Israel's perception that it can join the EU also harms the future development and upgrading of the relationship. Indeed recognition by Israeli and European officials that Israel cannot, and should not, advocate for membership of the EU, and instead should work on developing extensive cooperation agreements of is a basic starting point for the strengthening, and upgrading Israeli-EU relations.

The Israeli perception that good relations with the EU are not critical for Israel causes it particular harm. Not only does the Israeli economy and significant parts of its research and technology depend on cooperation with the EU, but Europe's standing in global affairs, in security policies, together with its desire to be more involved in the Middle East and in the Mediterranean, is likely to remain strong. As the EU's 2003 Security Strategy paper explains:

> As a union of 25 states with over 450 million people producing a quarter of the world's Gross National Product (GNP), and with a wide range of instruments at its disposal, the European Union is inevitably a global player. . . . The increasing convergence of European interests and the strengthening of mutual solidarity of the European Union makes us a more credible and effective actor. Europe should be ready to share the responsibility for global security and in building a better world.[32]

As for the Middle East conflict itself, the European Security Strategy paper considers the Middle East conflict as a violent conflict that persists on Europe's borders and threatens regional stability. The paper further emphasizes that the "resolution of the Arab/Israeli conflict is a strategic priority for Europe. . . . The European Union must remain engaged and ready to commit resources to the problem until it is solved."[33] The perceived difference in Israeli attitude toward Washington and Brussels may lessen as the Obama-led administration appears ready to work more harmoniously with the EU on the Middle East.

For any meaningful upgrade of Israeli-European relations, Israel needs to be cognizant that the EU is an emerging global actor, which has a potentially constructive role to play in shaping the geo-political and geo-strategic future of Israel. Europe intends to assume a key role in the management of international affairs:

> The European Union has the potential to make a major contribution, both in dealing with the threats and in helping realise the opportunities. An active and capable European Union would make an impact on a global scale. In doing so, it would contribute to an effective multilateral system leading to a fairer, safer and more united world.[34]

The role that the EU has chosen to play in the Lebanese crisis following the 2006 war, in defusing the Iranian nuclear crisis and in facilitating a cease-fire following the January 2009 Israeli incursion of the Gaza Strip, may prove that the EU is committed to its international role and may help Israel dispel its own perception with regard to the value of good political relations with Brussels.

The Israeli perception that EU policies toward Israel are deeply rooted and rigid and that large parts of the EU remain anti-Semitic is harder to dispel, given that there are voices in the EU that echo this view. In June 2008 former vice president of the European Commission and the current Italian foreign minister Franco Frattini ignited a storm at the meeting of the Annual Europe-Israel Dialogue. "I have to admit," declared Frattini, "if I look at the past, the EU has on some occasions taken an unbalanced stance toward Israel, even by making an unacceptable confusion between legitimate political criticism of Israel and intolerance against Jewish people that can become anti-Semitism."[35]

All Israelis interviewed for this study identified Europe's Muslims as a main source of the current rise of anti-Semitism in Europe. For them, in combination with growing Islamic populations in EU member states and some features of globalization, the results are radical versions of European anti-Semitism fused with anti-Zionism, anti-Israelism and anti-Americanism. All interviewees concluded that these culminate in the manifestation of a "new" expression of European anti-Semitism, superimposed on the traditional historical core of European anti-Semitism.

A View from Civil Society

In analyzing Israel's civil society, we conducted a study of 100 websites of major Israeli trade unions, academic institutions and NGOs (eight professional organizations and 92 academic, civil and community organizations). The Internet search was conducted between March and April 2008 and was based on a search for the terms "European Union" and "Europe." An additional component of this analysis consists of personal interviews with 20 leaders, directors and board members of Israel's leading trade unions, academic institutions and NGOs.

Thirty websites (30 percent) of the examined organizations made some reference to the EU/Europe in their websites. Five websites (5 percent) of the organizations made a reference on their homepage and 25 (25 percent) of them referred to the EU/Europe in other pages of their websites. Two percent of the organizations included a picture of the EU flag in their websites, one in a positive context and one in a negative context. In the thirty websites (30 percent) that mentioned the EU/Europe, we counted 134 items and links referring to the EU and 749 items and links referring to Europe. We then catalogued all items and links under 11 themes. The results are summarized in table 4.4.

On the face of it, the figure of 30 percent of organizations that made some kind of reference to the EU/Europe in their websites represents a significant quantitative measure. However, a qualitative analysis of these references produces a far less central role for the EU/Europe than the numbers might suggest.

It is important to emphasize that Israeli civil society is not unified in its approach to the EU. It is possible to divide Israeli civil society organizations into three categories: (i) organizations that are not concerned with the EU and for which the Union has no direct relevance to their work; (ii) organiza-

Table 4.4.   Distribution of Subjects and Links to EU/Europe by Theme in 100 Websites of Israeli Civil Society Organizations (Mar.–Apr. 2008)

Theme	Percentage
Human Rights	25
Professional Cooperation	12
Social	12
Health	9
Education	9
Economic and Trade	9
Financial Support	9
Middle East Peace Process	6
Israeli-EU Political Relations	3
Environment	3
Legal	3
Total	100%

Source: Pardo, Eskenazi and Kantz (2008).

tions that are aware that the EU can assist them but are not part of the group of organizations that enjoy the Union's financial support; and (iii) organizations that enjoy the Union's financial support. This third group includes left-wing and liberal civil society organizations that see the EU as a potential political and ideological partner. They believe that the Union respects the work of civil society even if their work is in tension with the policies of the Israeli government. As the director of one Israeli NGO explained, the EU exemplifies "how a democratic system should behave." Not surprisingly, these organizations perceive the EU as the global defender of human rights and as an independent global power.

Most of the Israeli NGOs are financially dependent on foreign sources for their funding, with the United States being the largest source of financial support for these organizations. However it is important to note that a majority of this financial support does not come directly from the U.S. government but rather from American Jewish communities. Echoing the implicit political fault lines between American and European funders, those civil society organizations that get their funding from the EU, and especially the organizations that work on Israeli-Palestinian/Arab issues, often stress that they "feel better with funds that come from the EU."

Unlike other Israeli sectors, many of the civil society organizations do not perceive the EU as an anti-Semitic entity; quite the opposite, most of them report that they never encountered any anti-Semitic behavior in their dealing with their European counterparts. For these organizations, the issue of anti-Semitism is not part of their agenda. Most Israeli NGOs stated that they would like Israel to strengthen relations with the EU; some of them would even like to see Israel as a full member of the EU. According to the director general of one of the largest Israeli civil society organizations, "if Israel were to join the EU, Israel would finally be a member of a family of nations that believe in human rights and in equality; a family of nations that fight for the protection of the environment. It is not that Europe is a perfect place, but European society is an enlightened society. Israeli EU membership will release us from our historical siege."[36]

Israeli Media Perceptions of the EU

Although newspaper circulations are currently in decline worldwide, leading newspapers still remain a major source of information for the general public, as well as for the country's elite and opinion leaders, playing a central role in forming foreign images and influencing the character of international relations. This is particularly true for Israel, where newspaper readership remains high. This section analyzes the content of the three leading national Hebrew newspapers, *Haaretz, Yedioth Ahronoth* and *Maariv*. These newspapers cover the Israeli ideological spectrum from left to right. While *Haaretz* targets a narrow readership mostly associated with the left, *Yedioth Ahronoth* and *Maariv* target a wider readership mostly associated with the centre and right of the Israeli ideological spectrum. They are the most widely read newspapers in Israel.[37] The analysis spans all news items in the printed editions of these newspapers between 1 October 2007 and 31 March 2008. A survey was carried out in which the names of the 27 EU member states or the terms "European Union" and/or "Europe" were mentioned in the headline or in the sub-headline, either in a value-laden context or in a descriptive, factual manner. We then used a simple matrix to catalog each news item according to the position it presented and whether the context was positive, negative, neutral or a simple presentation of general information. We also checked to see whether the news item covered Israel, Jewish communities/Holocaust/ anti-Semitism, foreign affairs, economy, security, culture, gossip or immigration. The results are summarized in tables 4.5–4.13.

Understanding the Media Findings

The number of news items relating to the EU and its member states varied greatly across Israel's three leading newspapers. *Haaretz* published 63.45 percent of all news items on Europe, while *Maariv* published 25.45 percent, and *Yedioth Ahronoth* published the remaining 11.1 percent. In terms of the content of the news items, it is noteworthy that most of the items do not overlap across the three newspapers and many news items tended to appear in only one paper.

Table 4.5. Press Coverage of the EU in Israel's Three Leading Newspapers (Oct. 2007–Mar. 2008)

Month	Haaretz	Yedioth Ahronoth	Maariv	Total
October 2007	71	14	46	131
November 2007	86	14	51	151
December 2007	88	15	44	147
January 2008	92	16	15	123
February 2008	84	10	28	122
March 2008	100	22	25	147
Total	521	91	209	821
Average Per Month	86.83	15.16	34.83	

Source: Pardo, Eskenazi and Kantz (2008).

Table 4.6. Number of Times the EU/Europe and EU Member States are Mentioned in *Haaretz* **(Oct. 2007–Mar. 2008)**

	POSITION				
EU/Europe/ Member State	Positive	Negative	Neutral	Informative	Total
EU/Europe	6	1	34	43	84
France	9	1	54	64	128
Germany	4	1	28	51	84
UK	3	0	29	39	71
Italy	3	1	22	16	42
Poland	4	0	9	6	19
Spain	0	0	9	17	26
Netherlands	0	0	7	8	15
Belgium	0	0	7	5	12
Austria	0	0	5	2	7
Sweden	0	0	2	5	7
Cyprus	0	0	5	2	7
Denmark	0	0	2	5	7
Ireland	2	0	2	2	6
Greece	0	1	2	2	5
Other EU MS	2	2	8	16	28
Total	33	7	225	283	

Source: Pardo, Eskenazi and Kantz (2008).

In its coverage of the EU and the individual member states, *Haaretz* focused more on internal affairs, foreign relations, Israel, the European Jewish communities, the Holocaust and anti-Semitism. In many cases *Haartez* published articles published by its own journalists; in other cases the newspaper published translated articles that were originally published in the *New York Times* and the *International Herald Tribune*. The news items published by *Haaretz* tended to be longer as well as more substantive and analytical than those published by *Maariv* and *Yedioth Ahronoth*.

The news items in *Maariv* and *Yedioth Ahronoth* were shorter and more superficial. For example, on 11 March 2008 *Yedioth Ahronoth* published a news item titled "Carla's Wine and Secret," which focuses on president Sarkozy's personal life and carried a large picture of Carla Bruni along with details of her personal life. It was only in the final paragraph that any reference was made to Sarkozy's policy positions. Another example relates to Muammar Qadhafi's visit to Paris. On 29 October 2007 *Yedioth Ahronoth* published an article entitled "Paris Gets Ready: Qadhafi Brings His Tent with Him." The article focused on the location of Qadhafi's tent and, again, only in last paragraph discussed the political and economic implications of this visit.

Table 4.7. Coverage in *Haaretz* of EU/Europe and EU Member States by Theme (Oct. 2007–Mar. 2008)

EU/Europe/ Member State	Israel	Jewish Communities, Holocaust, Anti-Semitism	External Affairs (excluding Israel)	Internal Affairs	Economy	Security	Culture	Immigration	Gossip
				THEME					
EU/Europe	5	2	31	18	14	3	3	2	0
France	15	9	39	35	0	6	9	5	16
Germany	22	26	16	14	0	7	4	6	0
UK	9	7	16	28	1	1	3	0	5
Italy	0	2	1	32	1	0	4	2	0
Poland	0	4	3	9	0	2	0	0	0
Spain	3	0	3	17	0	0	2	1	0
Netherlands	1	3	0	6	0	0	0	5	0
Belgium	0	2	0	9	0	0	0	1	0
Austria	0	1	0	2	0	2	0	1	1
Sweden	2	1	0	3	0	0	0	1	0
Cyprus	2	0	0	5	0	0	0	0	0
Denmark	0	0	0	3	0	0	0	3	0
Ireland	0	0	0	3	0	0	0	3	0
Greece	0	0	1	3	0	0	0	1	0
Other EU MS	2	4	2	8	3	0	2	3	0
Total	61	61	112	195	19	21	27	34	22

Source: Pardo, Eskenazi and Kantz (2008).

Table 4.8.   Number of Times the EU/Europe and EU Member States are Mentioned in *Yedioth Ahronoth* **(Oct. 2007–Mar. 2008)**

EU/Europe/ Member State	POSITION				
	Positive	Negative	Neutral	Informative	Total
EU/Europe	1	1	0	2	4
France	3	2	4	24	33
Germany	2	4	1	3	10
UK	1	0	1	4	6
Italy	0	1	5	2	8
Poland	2	0	0	2	4
Other EU MS	2	1	1	4	8
Total	11	9	12	41	

Source: Pardo, Eskenazi and Kantz (2008).

The percentage of news items mentioning the EU/Europe was much greater in *Haaretz* (16.12 percent of all news items published in *Haaretz*) compared with *Yedioth Ahronoth* (4.4 percent of all news items published in *Yedioth Ahronoth*) and *Maariv* (2.4 percent of all news items published in *Maariv*). It is important to note that the Treaty of Lisbon was signed during the period surveyed, yet this event attracted little attention. *Haaretz* published three news items on the Treaty; both *Yedioth Ahronoth* and *Maariv* published only one item each. When the papers did pay attention to the Treaty of Lisbon, they focused either on Poland (*Haaretz* highlighted the role that Poland played during the negotiation process) or on the new function of the president of the European Council (*Yedioth Ahronoth* and *Maariv*).

Out of the 27 EU member states, France is mentioned the most often by the Israeli newspapers. The focus of the news coverage was more on the personal life of president Sarkozy. While 36 percent and 38 percent of the news items published in *Yedioth Ahronoth* and *Maariv* (respectively) focused on France, a majority of them were dedicated to pure gossip regarding his personal life.

Haaretz, too, focused on France more than on any other EU member state during the said period (25 percent of the news items), but most of these items covered French foreign and domestic affairs (30.5 and 27.4 percent, respectively). Next to France, Germany received the most attention in Israel's three leading newspapers, with 14.74 percent of all news items referring to Germany. In *Yedioth Ahronoth* 90 percent of the news items on Germany related also to Israel, European Jewish communities, the Holocaust or European anti-Semitism. In *Haaretz* 57.14 percent of the news items did so, and in *Maariv* 48.15 percent mentioned Germany in one of these contexts.

Table 4.9. Coverage in *Yedioth Ahronoth* of EU/Europe and EU Member States by Theme (Oct. 2007–Mar. 2008)

EU/Europe/ Member State	Israel	Jewish Communities, Holocaust, Anti-Semitism	External Affairs (excluding Israel)	Internal Affairs	Economy	Security	Culture	Immigration	Gossip
EU/Europe	4	1	3	5	1	4	0	1	0
France	3	3	7	8	0	2	2	1	14
Germany	5	4	1	1	0	1	0	0	0
UK	1	1	0	0	0	1	0	0	2
Italy	0	0	0	7	0	0	0	1	0
Poland	1	0	0	3	0	0	0	0	0
Other EU MS	0	3	0	3	0	0	0	1	1
Total	14	12	11	27	1	8	2	4	17

Source: Pardo, Eskenazi and Kantz (2008).

Table 4.10.   Number of Times the EU/Europe and EU Member States are Mentioned in *Maariv* (Oct. 2007–Mar. 2008)

EU/Europe/ Member State	POSITION				
	Positive	Negative	Neutral	Informative	Total
EU/Europe	2	0	1	2	5
France	3	4	12	60	79
Germany	6	3	5	13	27
UK	2	0	8	26	36
Italy	0	2	1	4	7
Poland	1	2	1	9	13
Other EU MS	1	2	6	23	32
Total	15	13	34	137	

Source: Pardo, Eskenazi and Kantz (2008).

The KAS and Pardo 2009 national survey of Israeli attitudes toward the EU and its member states also reveals that Germany holds a very favorable image among Israelis, with 65 percent of those surveyed expressing their wish to see a more dominant German role within the EU. Not surprisingly, Germany's chancellor, Angela Merkel, comes out as one of the most popular leaders in Israel, with ratings of 56 percent favorable as opposed to 6 percent unfavorable.[38]

Analysis of the Media Data

One of the initial assumptions of this media survey was that the image of the EU would be dominated by either European attitudes toward Israel, European Jewish communities/anti-Semitism or economic themes. It was assumed that the Israeli media would frame the EU as an "economic power," a "political power of weakness" and as an anti-Jewish entity. Yet the first two parts of this assumption proved to be incorrect. The findings reveal that the coverage by Israel's three leading newspapers during the six-month period surveyed focused on the EU as "a powerful political system," and sometimes even "a power of passive aggression"[39] acting internally and externally. Paradoxically, the EU is framed as a marginal economic power with an anti-Jewish character.

It is interesting to point out that the EU's internal policies and member states' domestic affairs received the largest share of media attention—34.10 percent of all news items. The second most visible media framing of the EU was around the Union's external affairs—16.80 percent of the sampled news items.

Table 4.11. Coverage in *Maariv* of EU/Europe and EU Member States by Theme (Oct. 2007–Mar. 2008)

				THEME					
EU/Europe/ Member State	Israel	Jewish Communities, Holocaust, Anti-Semitism	External Affairs (excluding Israel)	Internal Affairs	Economy	Security	Culture	Immigration	Gossip
EU/Europe	1	0	0	1	2	0	0	4	0
France	4	9	11	20	1	5	5	4	22
Germany	3	10	0	5	0	1	0	1	0
UK	0	2	1	11	1	2	5	2	5
Italy	1	0	0	5	0	1	1	0	0
Poland	1	6	1	3	0	1	0	0	0
Other EU MS	1	7	2	13	1	2	2	5	0
Total	11	34	15	58	5	12	13	16	27

Source: Pardo, Eskenazi and Kantz (2008).

Table 4.12. Summary: Coverage of EU/Europe and EU Member States in Israel's Three Leading Newspapers by Theme (Oct. 2007–Mar. 2008)

EU/Europe/ Member State	Israel	Jewish Communities, Holocaust, Anti-Semitism	External Affairs (excluding Israel)	Internal Affairs	Economy	Security	Culture	Immigration	Gossip
				THEME					
EU/Europe	10	3	34	24	17	7	3	7	0
France	22	21	57	63	1	13	16	10	52
Germany	30	40	17	20	0	9	4	7	0
UK	10	10	17	39	2	4	8	2	12
Italy	1	2	1	44	1	1	5	3	0
Poland	2	10	4	15	0	3	0	0	0
Other EU MS	11	21	8	75	4	4	6	25	2
Total	86	107	138	280	25	41	42	54	66

Source: Pardo, Eskenazi and Kantz (2008).

Table 4.13. Summary: Number of Times the EU/Europe and EU Member States are Mentioned in Israel's Three Leading Newspapers (Oct. 2007–Mar. 2008)

EU/Europe/ Member State	POSITION				
	Positive	Negative	Neutral	Informative	Total
EU/Europe	9	2	35	47	93
France	15	7	70	148	240
Germany	12	8	34	67	121
UK	6	0	38	69	113
Italy	3	4	28	22	57
Poland	7	2	10	17	36
Other EU MS	7	6	56	91	160
Total	59	29	271	461	

Source: Pardo, Eskenazi and Kantz (2008).

While our initial assumption was that the Israeli media would take a neutral to negative approach toward the EU with regard to internal and external affairs, the findings reveal that Israel's three leading newspapers took a neutral or positive stance either. In 89.15 percent of all sampled news items the media presented the Israeli readers with a neutral position and in 7.19 percent of all sampled news items the media presented readers with a positive position. In only 3.53 percent of the items the Israeli media clearly took a negative position.

As discussed above, based on the general public feeling as well as statements by political elites regarding anti-Semitism in the EU, our initial assumption was that the image of the EU in the Israeli media would be framed by questions concerning Jewish communities, the Holocaust and European anti-Semitism and that the Union and its member states would be perceived as anti-Jewish entities. This assumption proved correct. This chapter shows that representation of the EU as an anti-Semitic entity received the third-largest share of media attention—13.03 percent of all news items.

These figures are troubling and go against a positive trend across the EU. As reports commissioned by the EU's Agency for Fundamental Rights (FRA) on the issue of anti-Semitism in the EU since 2002 reveal, although the number of violent anti-Semitic acts in the EU grew dramatically between 2002 and 2004, it steadily decreased until December 2008, after which it went up again, most probably in response to Israel's incursion of the Gaza Strip. Despite this encouraging trend, this chapter shows that Israel's three leading newspapers framed the Union as an entity with an anti-Jewish bias.

Explaining the frequency of news items on the Holocaust and European anti-Semitism, some of the foreign news editors of these dailies admitted that the decision to report extensively on anti-Semitic incidents in Europe and on the Holocaust was "simply because anti-Semitism and Holocaust sell newspapers in Israel." And often news items on anti-Semitism and the Holocaust were placed prominently on the front page. Notwithstanding this anti-Semitic image, the Union and its member states were portrayed as possessing democratic values, advocates for human rights, leading aid donors and active international negotiators on the Iranian nuclear crisis.

Conclusion

This chapter has examined images and perceptions of the EU across a broad spectrum of the Israeli society. It has also provided empirical material on Israelis' attitudes toward the EU. The chapter has revealed that Israelis hold three major perceptions about the EU. First, that the Union represents a hospitable framework for Israeli accession, and therefore that Israel could and should join the EU within the foreseeable future. This Israeli perception is driven by Israelis' hopes, desires and expectations of joining the Union. Second, which might be said to be contradictory to the first perception, is that good political relations with the EU are not really essential for Israel. The third fundamental perception, which follows from the second and accentuates the tension with the first, is that anti-Israeli attitudes and geostrategic views detrimental to the security of Israel are deeply rooted in the EU. Underlying this perception are Israeli feelings that large parts of the EU are anti-Semitic.

However problematic some of these perceptions and images might be, we should not lose sight of the fact that they play a critical role in relations between Israel and Europe. If Israel wants to continue developing and upgrading its relations with the EU, however, it should make much more of an effort to understand, and in some cases even dispel, its (mis)perceptions and images of the EU. The same responsibility also lies, of course, on the European side. While this chapter did not examine European perceptions and images of Israel, there is no reason to think that they deserve any less attention. As François Duchêne cautions us: "Israel can never be wholly foreign to [. . .] Europeans . . . Jews are so much part of the fabric of European history and contemporary life that relations with Israel must, in some sense, be an extension of folk memories on both sides."[40] And without understanding these memories, it will be difficult to address the perceptions and images on which the future of Israeli-European relations ultimately lies.

CHAPTER FIVE

Integration without Membership
A *Future* Model *for*
Israeli–European Union Relations

"Nothing is possible without men; nothing is lasting without institutions."

—Jean Monnet, 1978

A Need to Develop a Strong Institutional Foundation

Shortly before Germany took over the EU Presidency in the first half of 2007, Israel convinced the German government that the EU should revisit the 1994 Essen declaration. At the Essen heads of state meeting of December 1994 Europe's leaders had determined that Israel should enjoy a "*special status*" in its relations with the EU. Yet neither Israel nor Europe had given much thought in the intervening years to what this "*special status*" might actually entail in practice.

In response to this Israeli request, Israel and the EU established, in March 2007, the so-called "Reflection Group." This group was charged with examining various areas in which cooperation between Israel and the EU might be enhanced. Based on the preliminary findings of the Reflection Group, the EU-Israel Association Council met in Luxembourg on 16 June 2008 and decided to intensify the scope of relations between Israel and the EU. As was discussed in chapter 3, the upgrading of Israel's ties with the EU would

---

This chapter draws on a study conducted under the EuroMeSCo Network and an earlier version of it was published as a *EuroMeSCo Paper*.

revolve around three separate spheres: (i) promoting political cooperation through increased meetings between government ministers, senior officials and parliamentarians from both sides and the institutionalization of an Israeli-EU diplomatic dialogue; (ii) Israeli participation in European agencies, working groups and programs—with a view to achieving greater convergence toward the EU *acquis communautaire*; (iii) Israel's integration into the European Single Market.

In December 2008, the EU reaffirmed in Brussels its determination to upgrade its relations with Israel and issued a set of guidelines for strengthening its political dialogue with Israel. The Brussels guidelines called for inter alia: convening ad hoc summits at the level of heads of state and government as well as three meetings a year at the foreign minister level; allowing for each EU Presidency to invite, on an ad hoc basis, the director general of Israel's Ministry of Foreign Affairs to one of the meetings held during its term of office; providing for hearings of Israeli experts by Council working parties and committees; encouraging Israeli integration and involvement in multilateral fora; and intensifying inter-parliamentary dialogue.[1]

The Luxembourg statement and the Brussels guidelines offer Israel the opportunity to develop a closer relationship with Europe. Yet for all its desire to be a part of the European project, Israel has yet to develop a strategic vision of its desired relationship with the EU. The absence of any Israeli strategic thinking toward the EU has been noted within Europe. Benita Ferrero-Waldner, the EU commissioner for external relations, pointed out in a public lecture in Jerusalem that, "we [Europeans] strongly sense that Israel has not yet made up its mind how to work with us."[2] The same criticism can equally be leveled at Europe.

There is a pressing need to develop a stronger institutional foundation to support the upgrading of Israeli-EU relations. Without a stronger institutional framework there is a real risk that the process of upgrading Israeli-European relations will disintegrate into empty declarations and meaningless political exercises. The success of the process of upgrading Israel's ties to the EU demands that Israel and the EU craft a model to govern their future relationship. This chapter addresses that challenge. It presents a new institutional structure for the governing of Israel's future relations with the EU, the "Euro-Israeli Partnership" (EIP).

Some Principles for the Euro-Israeli Partnership

The Euro-Israeli Partnership is a new model for aligning Israel with the EU that is below the level of full EU membership. The EIP would open up new perspectives for Israel in terms of economic integration and cooperation, and would support Israel's aspiration to be incorporated into European economic and social structures. The EIP promises to deepen the process of approximating Israeli legislation, norms and standards to those of the Union. It should be emphasized that the EIP is not a mere stepping-stone to Israeli EU membership. Rather, it is a novel form of association and cooperation that could lead to a significant upgrade of Israeli-European relations, first and foremost in economic terms, but also in the political, research, as well as cultural and social/human fields. As such, the EIP provides a viable and practical framework within which Israel can pursue its wish of becoming a significant participant in the European integration project.

The proposed EIP model is based on the premise that a closer partnership between Israel and the EU would benefit both sides and would contribute to the overall improvement of mutual understanding and trust. The proposed model rejects the logic of the European Neighborhood Policy (ENP) and draws on the aim of the ENP to remain sufficiently flexible to allow individual partners to self-differentiate according to their political situation, level of ambition with regard to the EU, reform agenda and achievements, and level of socio-economic development. It could also serve as model for all ENP partner countries and may represent an appealing alternative to EU membership for other ENP partners.

Since its establishment, the EEC has searched for models for developing closer relations with non-EU member states. Referring to this issue, Walter Hallstein, the first president of the European Commission, stated on many occasions that: "[the links with a non-member country] can be anything between full membership minus 1 percent and a trade and cooperation agreement plus 1 percent."[3]

In like manner, in his June 2008 report on the European Commission's 2007 enlargement strategy paper, Elmar Brok, former chairman of the European Parliament's Foreign Affairs Committee, argued that the EU needed to develop "something between the European Neighbourhood Policy and full-fledged membership."[4] On this basis, in July 2008 the European Parliament (EP) adopted a resolution in which the Parliament took the view that "the conceptual, political and legal gap existing between the EU's Enlargement Strategy and its Neighbourhood Policy needs to be filled" in order to respond to the expectations of the Union's neighbors. Regarding those neighboring countries that, at present, do not enjoy the prospect of EU membership, but at the same time fulfill certain democratic and economic conditions, the resolution provides that:

> the EU should establish an area based on common policies covering, in particular, the rule of law, democracy and human rights, foreign and security policy

cooperation, economic and financial issues, trade, energy, transport, environmental issues, justice, security, migration, visa-free movement and education; [the European Parliament] . . . is also convinced that the common policies referred to above should be shaped jointly with the participating countries on the basis of specific decision-making mechanisms, and should be underpinned by adequate financial assistance. . . . [the European Parliament] recalls that, as a first step, these relations should translate themselves into the establishment of a Free Trade Area, to be followed by closer relations along the lines of a European Economic Area Plus (EEA +), of a European Commonwealth or of specific regional cooperation frameworks.[5]

The "special closer relations" with non-EU member states have also been inferred by a ruling of the European Court of Justice (ECJ). In its *Meryem Demirel* case the ECJ observed that the Community may conclude "an agreement creating special, privileged links with a non-member country." While the ECJ refrained from elaborating the substance of these "privileged links" with the non-member country, the Court's statement suggests that the relations should be based on more than just a regular trade agreement.[6]

Legal Foundations of the Euro-Israeli Partnership
The origins of the EIP can be found in the Barcelona Process, the EU-Israel Association Agreement, the ENP, the EU-Israel Action Plan, the Luxembourg statement of June 2008 and the Brussels guidelines of December 2008, and should be seen as the result of the long maturation of Israeli-European relations. From the point of view of both Israel and the EU, the EIP would fall within the legal category of an "association." The key article, Article 188 M of the Treaty of Lisbon (Article 310 of the Treaty Establishing the European Community [TEC]; Article 217 of the Treaty on the Functioning of the European Union [TFEU]), offers the fundamental legal basis of the EIP. Article 188 M states that: "The Community may conclude with one or more third countries or international organisations agreements establishing an association involving reciprocal rights and obligations, common action and special procedure."

A further legal source for the EIP is Article 7a of the Treaty of Lisbon (new Article 8 of the Treaty on European Union [TEU]). This article calls for the development of a "special relationship" with neighboring countries of the EU, including Israel. Although Article 7a uses different terms from Article 188 M, it has almost the same legal consequences. It states that:

1. The Union shall develop a special relationship with neighbouring countries, aiming to establish an area of prosperity and good neighbourliness, founded

on the values of the Union and characterised by close and peaceful relations based on cooperation.

2. For the purposes of paragraph 1, the Union may conclude specific agreements with the countries concerned. These agreements may contain reciprocal rights and obligations as well as the possibility of undertaking activities jointly.

Both Articles 188 M and 7a permit the development of an "association" or a "special relationship" that involves reciprocal rights and obligations as well as joint/common actions and special procedures. The articles are intentionally vague as to the content of each "association" or "special relationship." The EIP is legally based on the vagueness of Articles 188 M and 7a and on the flexibility that they allow for the development of Israeli-European relations. Being a tailor-made partnership, the EIP is designed to suit the interests and the needs of both Israel and the EU. Given that EU membership is restricted only to European states, the EIP model would entail less than full EU membership but more than the current EU-Israel Association Agreement/Action Plan.

A central component of the EIP is its permanency, and both Articles 188 M and 7a allow and imply a long-term relationship. This is further implied by Article 188 L(2) of the Treaty of Lisbon (Article 300(7) of the TEC; Article 216 of the TFEU), which stipulates that all international agreements concluded between the EU and one or more third countries or international organizations "are binding upon the institutions of the Union and on its Member States." And indeed, in practice all the Association Agreements and Partnership and Cooperation Agreements between the Union and non-EU member states are concluded for unlimited or for renewable periods.

A further component of the EIP is the "common action" or "joint activities" (Articles 188 M and 7a). In the *Meryem Demirel* case the ECJ affirmed that in the context of the "special, privileged links" with the EU, the non-member country "must, at least to a certain extent, take part in the Community system." It follows then, that any "common action" or "joint activities" should be in line with the Union's objectives. These actions can cover any area under the competence of the Community and above all they must depend on the interests of the two partners. In the Union's jargon, the partnership would be of a "mixed agreement" nature, namely a partnership that covers areas under Community external competences and national competences. An additional feature of the EIP is its institutional framework. The EIP would be equipped with its own institutional system. By using the term "special procedures," Article 188 M implies the creation of an institutional apparatus for the implementation of the agreement. It also follows that the "special procedure" should be an extraordinary one.[7]

Objectives of the Euro-Israeli Partnership

The principal objective of the EIP is to foster the continuous strengthening of economic trade and political relations between the two parties, with a view to creating a "homogeneous partnership economic area." The objective of homogeneity is a cornerstone of the EIP and would guarantee that Israel closely follows the *acquis communautaire* and its associated monitoring system. The EIP would extend the internal market and develop some of the existing EU policies geared toward Israel. More specifically, the partnership would be based on the *acquis communautaire* concerning the Four Freedoms. Nevertheless, it is expected that for political reasons the "freedom of movement of persons" will touch a raw nerve in Israel and that Israel would therefore prefer not to implement this particular freedom in the short term. As such, the EIP should stipulate the extension to the partnership of this freedom, subject to a favorable change in the region's political situation.

The fundamental means through which the partnership's objectives could be achieved are the Four Freedoms, competition rules, and Israeli-EU cooperation agreements in several key areas. An extension of the Community's common market rules to Israel would help in attaining the economic goal of the partnership. The creation of a "homogenous partnership economic area" could be made possible through the application of common rules and the updating of new Community rules. As such, the EIP has the potential to become a very dynamic partnership since it would follow closely major developments in the EU, and integrate relevant Community legislation on a periodical basis. In other words, Israel would face a cardinal challenge of incorporating the relevant parts of the *acquis communautaire* included in the partnership.

The Institutional Framework of the Euro-Israeli Partnership

Israeli-European relations do not currently reflect the notion of an increasingly closer partnership. The relationship must achieve a higher level of integration by strengthening the sense of a close partnership. Moreover, in view of the "special procedures" under Article 188 M of the Treaty of Lisbon, and given the dynamism and the wide scope of the EIP, it would prove unwise to rely solely on the current loose Euro-Mediterranean Partnership/ Union for the Mediterranean-European Neighborhood Policy institutional framework of Israeli-European relations—namely, the Association Council, the Association Committee and its subcommittees and working groups (see figure 5.1). To assure its full implementation and its future development, the EIP would have to reinforce the current loose institutional framework and eventually establish a new institutional system.

In order to become a proactive partnership that would engage Israel and the EU in an equitable manner, the institutional framework of the EIP

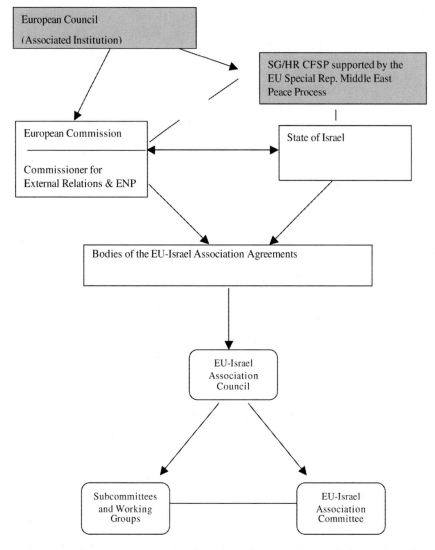

Figure 5.1. The Current Institutional Framework of Israeli-EU Relations (EMP/UfM-ENP Framework)

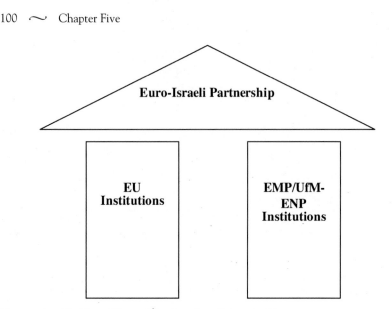

Figure 5.2. The Two Pillars of the Euro-Israeli Partnership

should be based on two pillars: the EU institutions, and the light institutional framework of the EMP/UfM-ENP (see figure 5.2).

Some new common institutions are however needed, especially for joint-decision making and for the settlement of legal disputes. It is hoped that the EIP institutional framework will reflect the partnership's principle of cooperation, establishing the EIP into a mechanism for consultations and negotiations and limiting the EU-centric character of existing Israeli-European economic and trade relations (see figure 5.3).[8]

The EIP Council

Meeting at the ministerial level twice a year, the EIP Council would stand as the highest political body of the partnership and would consist of members of the EU Council, the EU Commission and the relevant representative of the Israeli government. Based on the current Association Council, the new EIP Council would provide the political impetus necessary for the implementation of the EIP objectives, and would establish the guidelines for the work of the EIP Joint Monitoring Committee. For administrative and organizational purposes, the EIP Council would be led for a set period of time (for example, twelve months) by a rotating chairmanship headed by either a member of the European Council or a member of the Israeli government. Decisions by the EIP Council would be taken by agreement between Israel and the Union. Under this new model of Israeli-European relations, with its freshly established mechanism and powers, the EIP Council would fully reflect the equality, the negotiating, decision-making and decision-shaping character of the partnership.

The EIP Joint Monitoring Committee

Based on the work of the current Association Committee, the new EIP Joint Monitoring Committee would be an independent committee charged with administering the day-to-day business of the partnership and ensuring that the parties fulfill their EIP commitments. The Committee would decide on new legislation to incorporate into the partnership. Meeting on a monthly basis it would consist of an equal number of high officials and senior diplomats from the European Council, EU Commission and the Israeli government (for example, 5+5). The Committee would also be able to convene informal meetings to respond to urgent situations. As with the EIP Council, the Committee would be managed by a rotating chairmanship and decisions would be taken by agreement between Israel and the Union. To assist in its task, the Committee would be entitled to establish subcommittees and working groups.

The EIP Joint Monitoring Committee would act as an extension of the Council Presidency and would provide it the support required for all Council's activities. The Committee would also assist the Presidency in preparation of all meetings of the EIP Council. In addition, the Committee would ensure that all EIP institutions would act in conformity with EIP guidelines and would report directly to the EIP Council. The Committee would also be responsible for preparing the annual report on the activities of the EIP.

The EIP Parliamentary Committee

The EIP Parliamentary Committee would be based on the current European Parliament Delegation for Relations with Israel and the Knesset Delegation for Relations with the EP, and would be composed of an equal number of members of the EP and the Knesset (for example, 10+10). The Committee would act through dialogue and debate to ensure better understanding between Israel and the Union in the areas covered by the partnership. The Committee would have the right to express its views on all matters relating to the EIP and in particular would monitor the "homogenous partnership economic area." Although the Committee would hold no decision-making powers, it would be entitled to adopt resolutions and submit reports and recommendations to the EIP Council, with a view to achieving the objectives of the EIP.

The EIP Parliamentary Committee would be an authentic institution with a consultative capacity. Its creation should assist Israeli-European parliamentarians in meeting some of the social, legal, and economic challenges which the EIP is expected to face. The Committee would further explore subjects addressed during the meetings of the EIP Council, promote partnership-building measures and would contribute to the development of the EIP institutions.

The EIP Court of Conciliation and Arbitration

Institutional solutions to political partnership and integration must be conceived within a framework of law. To a large degree, political partnership and integration really means legal partnership and integration. Not only is political partnership and integration brought to life by means of a corresponding integration of laws, but the latter is also an expression of the particular form of political partnership and integration being pursued. More importantly, however, the extent of political integration can be determined through an evaluation of the level of legal integration in evidence.

Once the function of law in political partnership and integration is understood, the role potentially played by the judiciary in cementing political partnership and integration can hardly be questioned. Political partnership and integration can exist without courts, just as law could exist without them. However, for the same reason that courts are vital in the administration of justice, courts are also important in the process of political partnership and integration. Just as courts control and assure the administration of law, they also control and assure the observance of those political decisions that underlie the political partnership and integration in question.

The deepening of Israeli-European relations will depend on a close legislative cooperation and exchange of views. The EIP is liable to increase the instances in which arbitration will be required to settle disputes in the framework of the EIP. Moreover, since the EIP would possess its own limited legal system, which would be based on Community law, the institutionalization of judicial facilitation must take the form of a partnership court. The EIP Court would act by means of conciliation and, where appropriate, arbitration. Its rulings would be binding. To cut the Court's expenses, the Court would not be a permanent tribunal but rather a roster of conciliators and arbitrators from both sides. Accordingly, the Court would act as an ad hoc Conciliation Commission or an ad hoc Arbitral Tribunal, convening only when a dispute is submitted to it. In addition, Israeli courts would be allowed to ask the EIP Court for an advisory opinion on the interpretation of the partnership. National courts of EU member states would also be permitted to ask for preliminary rulings from the ECJ.

The conciliators and arbitrators must be persons whose independence is beyond doubt and who possess the qualifications required for appointment to the highest judicial offices in their respective countries or who are jurisconsults of recognized competence. The competence and integrity of the conciliators and arbitrators is crucial for several reasons. Obviously such qualities will have a positive effect on the soundness of the rulings and will also breed greater respect for the EIP Court in Israel, in all the EU member states, as well as in other EU institutions. The Court's conciliators and arbitrators would not receive instructions from their home countries, nor would they allow themselves to be influenced by political considerations or any other considerations that might prejudice their judicial work. There would be no dissenting opinions since the ruling of the EIP Court would always be presented as a single ruling. The deliberations would be secret so their details could be unknown to anyone but aside from those conciliators and arbitrators who voted. As such, any national bias would remain undisclosed.

The EIP would establish an obligatory conciliation procedure that would feed into a non-binding concluding report. If within thirty days, the partners failed to approve the conclusions presented, the report would be forwarded to the Arbitral Tribunal whose ruling would be binding. Finally, if a dispute in question concerned the interpretation of Community legislation relevant to the EIP, it would be possible to ask the ECJ to rule on the interpretation of the relevant legislation. The ECJ ruling would be binding.

The Israeli Standing Committee

For the management of its internal procedures, Israel would establish a Standing Committee responsible for decision-making procedures, administration and management of the partnership, as well as inter-ministerial coordination and consultation. The Committee would also facilitate the elaboration of decisions to be taken on the EIP level.

The Israeli Standing Committee would consist of representatives of all Israeli ministries, including representatives of all relevant institutions and agencies. The Standing Committee would meet regularly (possibly as frequently as on a monthly basis) at the level of high officials. In addition, the Committee would meet at a ministerial level if necessary. The Committee might set up subcommittees and working groups to assist it in all its tasks. The decisions and recommendations of the Standing Committee would be reached by a majority vote and in some cases would also require the approval of the Israeli government.

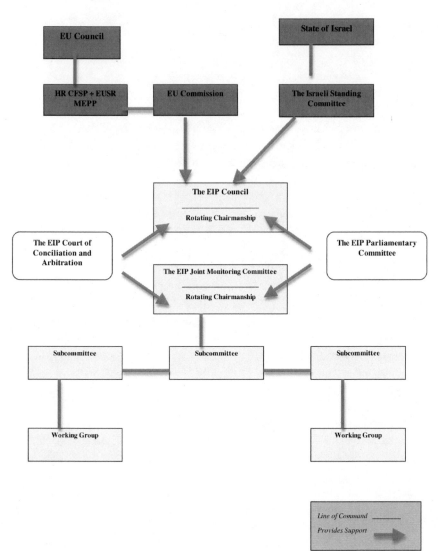

Figure 5.3.   The Proposed Institutional Structure of the Euro-Israeli Partnership

Decision-Shaping and Decision-Making Processes

Given that the EIP is based on the Union's legislation, the Union would continue to legislate using its own internal procedures. Any new Community legislation relevant to the EIP must be incorporated into the partnership upon a joint decision of both Israel and the Union. Israel would be able to participate in "decision-shaping" where the EU judges that the Community legislation is applicable to the EIP. In such cases, Israel would only be involved in the preparatory stages of the Union legislative process.

Under this process, once the European Commission has drafted new legislation in an area the EU judges to be relevant to the EIP, the Commission would notify Israel and would send it a copy of the draft proposal. If Israel wished to discuss the proposal, a preliminary exchange of views would take place in the EIP Joint Monitoring Committee. Furthermore, the European Commission would ensure participation of Israeli experts in the "Comitology Committees."[9] The Commission would also submit the views of the Israeli experts to the EU Council.

Once any pertinent Community legislation has been formally adopted by the Union's institutions, the EIP Joint Monitoring Committee would then decide on its incorporation of the legislation into the partnership. If accepted, the Committee would also examine whether there is a need for any technical amendments, transitional periods or derogations. Such legislative incorporation would be needed in order to guarantee the homogeneity of the EIP. The EIP Joint Monitoring Committee would finalize its decisions as soon as possible in order to allow a simultaneous application in the EU and the EIP.

A decision by the EIP Joint Monitoring Committee would be taken within a short period of time (for example, six months) following a referral to the Committee or from the date of entry into force of the Community legislation in question. All decisions to extend Community legislation also to the EIP would be published in a special "EIP Section" of the Official Journal of the EU. Translation into Hebrew would be published in a special "EIP Series" of the Official Gazette of the State of Israel-*Reshumot.*

Maintaining Homogeneity

The homogeneity objective is a cornerstone of the EIP and both partners would have to maintain uniform interpretation of the relevant provisions of the Community legislation. This means that the partnership would have its own limited legal system, which would be based on Community law. For the sake of homogeneity, all the relevant Community legislation would have to be interpreted in conformity with the relevant rulings of the ECJ without prejudice to the independence of all EIP institutions, including of course the EIP Court of Conciliation and Arbitration. Both the EIP Joint Monitoring Committee and the EIP Court of Conciliation and Arbitration would pay due account to the principles laid down by the relevant rulings of the ECJ. Finally, the Israeli courts would be allowed to ask the EIP Court of Concili- ation and Arbitration for an advisory opinion on the interpretation of the partnership.

To safeguard uniformity in the implementation and application of the partnership rules, the European Commission and the Israeli Standing Com- mittee would cooperate, exchange information and consult each other on surveillance policy issues and on individual cases. Both bodies would be re- sponsible for handling complaints from individuals. In cases of disagreements over a complaint, each institution would be allowed to refer the matter to the EIP Joint Monitoring Committee.

Implementing the Partnership

Israel and the EU would have to take all possible measures to ensure the fulfillment of the obligations arising out of the EIP. After the process of negotiating the EIP Agreement, both partners would need to adopt this accord and create the new institutions of the partnership. It is clear that Israel would have to adapt its domestic legislation in order to introduce the measures required to bring the Israeli legal system in conformity with its EIP obligations. This would imply a long transitional period and a heavy load of implementation work, mainly on the Israeli side, before the EIP Agreement can enter into force. As for the Union itself, it seems that, following Article 188 L(2) of the Treaty of Lisbon, the Union would not have to amend the *acquis communautaire* in order to comply with the EIP obligations, as inter- national agreements concluded by means of the procedure set out in Article 188 M of the Treaty of Lisbon are binding on the institutions of the Com- munity and its member states. As the ECJ has described it: "The provisions of such agreements and measures adopted by the institutions set up by such agreements become an integral part of the Community legal order when they enter into force."[10]

Potential European and Israeli Support for the EIP Model

While the proposed EIP model has not been presented to the leaderships of either Israel or the EU, there is ample evidence on both sides that they would support the logic behind it. In September 2007, the EU Commission orga- nized an international conference on the ENP, titled "Taking the Neigh- bourhood Policy Forward." In his opening address, president José Manuel Barroso, president of the European Commission, declared that:

The ENP is not, and never has been, a one-size-fits-all policy. There are as many variations of ENP as there are partners. We cannot and do not wish to ignore the differences between our partners. . . . With each of our ENP partners we craft a specific and unique relationship. . . . As the policy develops, this differentiation will become more pronounced. When we launched the policy, we had to make it clear that the offer on the table was the same for everyone, with no discrimination. But as we get further and further away from the starting line, I expect we will see a more and more varied landscape, with as many different types of relationship developing as we have partners, but always within the common framework of the ENP.[11]

The European Commission has adopted a similar line of thinking. In a Communication on "A Strong European Neighbourhood Policy" issued in December 2007, it argued that:

The ENP includes very different countries in a single policy. The EU offer of deeper relations is the same for all partners. However, the country-specific approach within the ENP provides for flexibility and differentiation, and there are as many possible responses as there are partner countries, according to each partner's political situation, its level of ambition with regard to the EU, its reform agenda and achievements, and its level of socio-economic development. The enhanced agreement currently being negotiated with Ukraine, the ongoing discussions with Morocco on an "advanced status" and with Israel on an upgrading of relations demonstrate this differentiation. The further the policy evolves, the more pronounced this differentiation will become.[12]

The logic of the EIP model is also likely to attract interest within Israeli policy-making circles. In the past, prime minister Binyamin Netanyahu expressed great interest in Israeli integration in the EU. In 2002, in his capacity as foreign minister, he said in a radio interview that Israel was considering joining the EU and that it would ask Italy for assistance in order to achieve this goal.[13] In his capacity as finance minister, Netanyahu stated in 2003 that Israel might consider joining the Eurozone. Deputy prime minister and minister of foreign affairs, Avigdor Liberman, has publicly announced his support for Israel's accession to the EU and NATO. In 2007, in his capacity as deputy prime minister and minister for strategic affairs, Liberman declared that "Israel's diplomatic and security goal must be clear: joining NATO and entering the EU."[14] Likewise, Liberman's party's (Yisrael Beytenu) platform ahead of the February 2009 general elections, stated that "one of the clear goals of Yisrael Beytenu is Israel's joining of the European Union and NATO."[15]

Further support for the logic behind the EIP can be evinced from official statements specifically addressing Israeli-European relations. In May 2007, two months after the establishment of the Israeli-EU Reflection Group, ambassador Yossi Gal, then the senior deputy director general of political affairs in the Israeli Ministry of Foreign Affairs, and now the director general of the ministry, declared that "the new model of Israeli-European relations should not follow a model that exists." In response the Commission's ambassador to Israel, Ramiro Cibrian-Uzal, immediately affirmed that "there should not be any reason why Israel should not have its own unique model for relations with the EU."[16] Finally, there would be strong support among Israelis for an enhanced institutional relationship with the EU. As has been shown in the previous chapter Israelis would like to see Israeli-European relations go even deeper than the proposed EIP model, with a solid majority supporting Israeli membership in the EU. In a survey from April 2009, 69 percent of those polled either "strongly supported" or "somewhat supported" the idea that Israel should join the EU.[17]

The pace of any upgrading of Israeli-European relations is ultimately dependent on developments in the Middle East peace process, and on the Israeli government's readiness to move toward a two-state solution. Positive progress in the Israeli-Palestinian context would result in the speeding up of negotiations over any upgrade in the near future and the potential implementation of the EIP, while negative developments are expected to lead to a suspension of this process.

Conclusion: Providing a Mechanism to Propel Israeli-European Relations

In order to create a genuine EU-Neighborhood space, there is a pressing need to strengthen the institutional foundation and structure of EU-neighbors relations in general and Israeli-European relations in particular. Otherwise, following Jean Monnet, "great ideas and principles either take firm shape in the form of institutions, or disappear into rhetoric and finally die." To be effective the European Neighborhood Policy should not be left to politicians and diplomats alone, a tattered flag to be waved during the meetings of the Association Councils and Association Committees. There is a real risk that, without solid institutional expression, the ENP will disintegrate into relatively meaningless political exercises rather than become a true Neighborhood Policy.

The structural relationship between the EU and its ENP partners needs to be altered, if the ENP is to attain its objectives. The EU-centric character of those relations and the current institutional structure does not reflect an ever-closer partnership between the EU and its neighbors under the ENP.

The relations between the EU and its neighbors should be urgently reshaped and institutionally restructured to more effectively identify and cultivate common interests and potential synergies. Such a task is a prerequisite if the ENP is ever going to evolve into anything other than expressions of European noblesse oblige. The current proposals to beef up the ENP are unlikely to suffice.

The Euro-Israeli Partnership offers such an institutional framework. It would provide the ENP with a mechanism to propel the partnership forward from the arena of declarations to one of implementation. The unique partnership proposed in this chapter could serve as a model and springboard from which the consolidation process of the "ring of friends surrounding the Union"[18] as suggested by Romano Prodi can begin to take shape. The EIP equips both the ENP and Israeli-European relations with partnership-building tools necessary to deliver greater political, commercial and functional cooperation.

The successful implementation of the EIP is admittedly a daring and immense challenge for both partners, and one which should not be underestimated. But if the EU and its member states are committed to the existence, survival and prosperity of Israel, and if Israel truly wishes, as Israeli leaders have declared, to "participate in the European integration process,"[19] then strengthening Israeli-European relations along the lines outlined in this chapter should be seriously considered.

CONCLUSION

~

Looking Back, Looking Forward

"Europe, that wonderful, murderous continent."

—Amos Oz, 2002

Over the past thirty years Israel and Europe have become increasingly closer. Today the balance sheet in terms of the wealth of personal and business connections that have been developed, the numerous joint cooperative ventures and the economic content of those ties is positive and solid.

Trade between the EU and Israel has flourished in the last decade. The EU is now Israel's most important trading partner. In 2008, 34 percent of Israeli imports, totaling about €16 billion (excluding diamonds), came from the EU, and 33 percent of Israeli exports, totaling about €12.5 billion (excluding diamonds), were directed to the European market. Israel is the Union's twenty-fifth major trading partner. EU imports and exports have grown successively in the past decade. However in 2008, EU imports from Israel fell by 1.4 percent (while they increased by 8.1 percent with the rest of the world) and EU exports to Israel decreased during the same period by 1.6 percent (while they increased by 5.4 percent with the rest of the world).[1]

The deepest level of cooperation lies in the field of scientific cooperation and in research and development. Since 1996, Israel has been the only non-European country fully associated with the EU's Framework Programs for Research and Technological Development (FP). Among the Associated Countries to the Seventh FP, Israel is the EU's third-largest partner, after Switzerland and Norway, in terms of the program's participation. Israel is an active member in the EU's FP and has proved to be a source of innovation in both basic and market-oriented research conducted in Europe, in particular in the areas of Information Communication Technology (ICT), health, environment, nanosciences, and Materials and New Production Technologies (NMP). The success rate of Israeli researchers goes far beyond the associated countries average.[2] By July 2009, over 3,310 proposals involving Israeli researchers were received under the Seventh Research Framework Programme (FP7). Of those 630 were accepted, with the EU contributing over €220 million.[3] The EU is now Israel's second-biggest source of research funding, after the Israel Science Foundation. Israel will contribute approximately €440 million to FP7 over the period 2007–2013. In July 2004 Israel and the EU signed an agreement that provides for cooperative activities on satellite navigation and timing in a wide range of sectors, notably science and technology, industrial manufacturing, service and market development, as well as standardization, frequencies and certification. Israel has also been invited by the EU to take part through a financial stakeholding in the Galileo Joint-Undertaking, the body responsible for the management of this first global civil satellite program.[4]

The links between Israel and Europe go beyond simply a matter of trade and scientific cooperation. Israelis are attracted to European history, tradition, lifestyle and culture and attach importance to the cultural and sporting links with Europe. Europe and its cities are a favored destination for Israeli holidaymakers. According to the Konrad-Adenauer-Stiftung (KAS) and Pardo 2007 and 2009 national surveys on Israelis' attitudes toward the EU and its member states, 48 percent of the Israeli population has visited Europe in the past three years. Despite the concerns over the increase in anti-Semitic incidents in Europe and the unease with European positions on the Middle East peace process, the Israeli public is favorably disposed toward Europe and a large part of the population attaches great importance to the strengthening of relations with the EU. As discussed in chapter 4, according to the KAS and Pardo 2007 and 2009 national surveys, 60 percent of the Israelis favor the EU. Even more surprising is the large number of Israelis that support the idea of Israel joining the EU. An overwhelming majority, 69 percent, of the Israeli public either "strongly supported" or "somewhat supported" the idea that Israel should join the EU. Israelis are also beginning to seek ways of acquiring European citizenship. With the 2005 and 2007 eastern enlargements of the EU, about 40 percent of Israelis are identified as eligible for EU citizenship, and many are taking up the new opportunity afforded to them.[5]

At the political level Israeli and European leaders have long stressed the importance of strengthening ties. As discussed in chapter 4, some Israeli politicians have even raised the prospect of Israel applying for membership in the EU, and of pegging the Israeli shekel to the Euro. In the past, such ideas were limited to the left wing of the Israeli political spectrum. This is no longer the case. The advocacy of closer ties with the EU now cuts across the political spectrum. Silvan Shalom, a leading figure in the Likud, made improving relations with Europe a priority when he became foreign minister in 2003. Tzipi Livni was a driving force behind Israel's push for upgrading ties with the EU, and placed great emphasis on securing European support for the Annapolis process. Avigdor Liberman, Israel's current foreign minister, has often referred to the necessity of Israel joining NATO and entering the EU. And Binyamin Netanyahu, who as prime minister in 1999 had denounced European leaders for their support of Palestinian statehood in the Berlin declaration, has suggested that Israel should consider linking its economic future to the Eurozone.

Statements by Israeli and European leaders have placed great emphasis on the depth of the friendship between their countries, frequently referring to their shared heritage, culture and values, and their common strategic interests. As discussed in chapter 3, this has led to a series of diplomatic initiatives over the past fifteen years aimed at improving Israel's formal standing with the EU. At the 1994 Essen heads of state meeting, European leaders tried to put some substance into those sentiments by declaring that Israel should be granted a "special status" in its relations with the EU. More recently, in November 2003, the EU announced that upgrading relations with Israel would be a top priority as part of its new Wider Europe Policy. And in June 2008, Europe's leaders agreed to work toward upgrading Israel's formal standing with the EU.

Yet Israeli-European relations have consisted of a number of conflicting trends that have resulted in the emergence of a highly problematic and volatile relationship: one characterized by a strong and ever increasing network of economic, cultural and personal ties yet marked, at the political level, by disappointment, bitterness and anger. On the one hand, Israel has displayed a genuine desire to strengthen its ties with Europe and to be included as part of the European project. On the other hand, Israelis are deeply suspicious of European policies, and are untrusting of Europe's intentions toward the Arab-Israeli conflict and to the region as a whole. As a result, Israel has been determined to minimize the EU's role in the peace process, and to deny it any direct involvement in the negotiations with the Palestinians.

Europe displays an equally ambivalent attitude concerning the nature of its ties with Israel. The EU talks of its desire to develop a "special relationship" with Israel and to afford Israel a separate standing from other countries in the Middle East. Yet it has failed to articulate what such a status might actually entail. Europeans want Israel to embrace the European project, to adopt its values and act according to those goals. At the same time, in its policies the EU treats Israel as an outsider. Europeans do not regard Israel as belonging fully to Europe and believe that Israel's future lies within the Mediterranean and the Middle East.

Without question, it is the friction over the peace process that has most soured Israeli-European relations, which have over the years become hostage to the vicissitudes of immediate events and specific developments (positive and negative) within the Arab-Israeli peace process. Many of the exchanges between Israel and the EU on the peace process have consisted of finger-pointing and apportioning blame, rather than finding areas of common ground. The discourse often appears to be more intent of addressing unfinished business from the past, ignoring the substantive links of trust that have been built up within European and Israeli business, scientific and security circles.[6]

European leaders and civil society have been frustrated by the lack of progress in the peace process. They have been resentful of the way in which Israel has marginalized the EU's role and angered that Israel does not recognize sufficiently that Europe holds genuine interest in securing stability in the region. They have argued strongly that the EU needs to be afforded a position commensurate with its global standing. Israel's (over)reliance on military measures to secure its defense is seen in Europe as disproportionate and in contravention to international law and serves as a contributory factor to the rising tensions in the region. For Europeans, Israel needs to be more cognizant of the human aspects of security, such as the respect for human rights, economic welfare and development, and not just its military aspects.

European criticisms of Israeli policies have often become amplified and are seen by Israel as ignoring Palestinian actions and intransigence. Israelis see Europe as weak on international terrorism and as unwilling to undertake the necessary measures to counter this threat. Futhermore, Israel has accused Europeans of not being sufficiently concerned about its security and as failing to acknowledge the policy dilemmas it faces in trying to protect its citizens from Palestinian terrorism and in preventing suicide attacks. In response to European criticisms of its policies, Israel has often been quick to point to the growth of anti-Semitism in Europe and the lack of genuine efforts by Europeans to undertake effective measures to counter this phenomenon, as a further indication of underlying European antipathy to Jewish concerns and interests, and by association, Israel's long-term security.

The differences between Israel and Europe are not simply over immediate policy choices but reflect a deeper clash over strategic culture. For many in

Israel, Europe has become a "lost continent." Israelis are disappointed that Europeans do not fully recognize Israel's hostile strategic environment, the nature of the short- and long-term threats it faces and the measures needed in order to counter those threats. Europe's projection of normative power and its stress on cooperative practices is dismissed in Israel as an expression of its weakness and of its lack of will and capacity to act on the global stage. Israelis see European emphasis on human security issues as hollow. They accuse Europe of being hypocritical and of failing to apply those standards—human rights, good governance, rule of law—in their dealings with the Arab world.

Recent years have witnessed a shift in Israeli thinking of the importance of multilateral security governance and a more nuanced view on human security issues. Eight years of fighting Palestinian insurgency, the seemingly endless cycle of action and reaction, the degeneration of the Palestinian political environment and the recent military campaigns in Lebanon and Gaza have led many in Israeli policy circles to question the ability of military force, by itself, to meet the security challenges Israel faces. There is growing realization within Israeli policy circles that multilateralism has become an essential, if not an inescapable, component of international life, and that multilateral cooperation provides domestic and international legitimacy, burden sharing and access to knowledge and information. This has resulted in the development of a strategic dialogue with the EU, a willingness to see an enhanced role for the Union in building up Palestinian security capacity, and a growing interest in upgrading its ties with NATO.[7] The EU has a critical role in fostering this new security discourse on and helping integrate Israel into multilateral security governance structures. Attitudes toward Europe within Israel have become entwined in and frequently manipulated by Israeli domestic politics over the peace process. This has resulted in negative consequences for Israeli-European relations. Those in Israel opposed to European views on the conflict accuse the EU of funding Palestinian groups associated with terrorism. They have presented European support for peace efforts, especially the funding of human rights NGOs and peace organizations, as indicative of an underlying hostility amongst Europeans toward the Jewish state, and reflective of a long-held bias toward the Arab world.[8] In contrast, those who share similar perceptions on the imperative and possibility for resolving the conflict have actively sought out European support and have encouraged an enhanced European role in the peace process. Almost exactly, those promoting Israeli-European relations or denigrating Europe's cause in Israel mirror this division of opinion on Europe's role in the peace process.

Israel and the EU have held a differing set of priorities, interests, and strategies toward the Arab-Israeli conflict. As discussed in chapter 1, those differences have brought Israel and Europe to loggerheads over the years and to periodic crises in their relationship. Those approaches can be divided into three broad areas: (i) the contours of a solution to the conflict, and specifically the need for a Palestinian state; (ii) the question of Palestinian representation; and (iii) the political process needed to resolve the conflict.

The past few years, however, have witnessed a growing convergence in Israeli and European strategies toward the conflict. Most notably, Israel, through its acceptance of the 2003 Roadmap, has endorsed the idea of the two-state solution to the Israeli-Palestinian conflict. Israel's leaders have spoken increasingly of the corroding effect of the occupation of Palestinian territories on Israeli society, and of the strategic necessity, if not the moral imperative, of withdrawing from the West Bank. Ariel Sharon's decision to unilaterally withdraw Israeli forces from Gaza in August 2005 and to dismantle Israeli settlements was widely supported by the Israeli public. The need to end Israel's occupation and establish a Palestinian state is now accepted by most sectors of Israeli society, though with varying degrees of enthusiasm. The acceptance of the two-state solution has led to a marked warming in Israeli-EU relations and, with it, the gradual acceptance by Israel of an enhanced European role in bringing the conflict to an end. In the past year, however, that convergence has shown signs of cracking, presenting the potential for renewed tensions and an erosion of Israeli-European relations.

While differences exist over the best strategies for its resolution, European states have been unified over the contours of a peace settlement for the last thirty years: a two-state solution based on the 1967 borders, a sharing of sovereignty in Jerusalem and an agreed-upon solution to the Palestinian refugee issue. The Venice declaration of June 1980 outlined a set of principles and diplomatic steps that needed to be taken in order to achieve a lasting resolution of the Palestinian question. Those principles have defined European positions ever since. But more critically, and to the anger of Israel, it called for the inclusion of the PLO in any future negotiating process. The call by European leaders for the inclusion of the PLO was a defining moment in Israeli discourse and in the public distrust of Europe as a potential mediator in the Arab-Israeli peace process. It signaled a low point in Israel's relations with the EU from which they have never fully recovered. The ferocity of Israel's response captures the impact that the declaration had on Israeli perceptions:

> Nothing will remain of the Venice Resolution but its bitter memory. The Resolution calls upon us, and other nations, to include in the peace process

the Arab S.S. known as "The Palestine Liberation Organization." . . . For a "peace," which would be achieved with the participation of that same organization of murderers, a number of European countries are willing to give guarantees, even military ones. . . . Any man of good will and any free person in Europe who would examine this document would see in it a Munich-like surrender, the second in our generation, to tyranic extortion.[9]

After the signing of the Oslo Accords in September 1993, the question of the PLO receded into the background, though Israel and the EU did clash over the political and diplomatic isolation imposed on Yasser Arafat by Israel during the al-Aqsa *intifada* in 2002. Although the EU tightened up its funding to the Palestinian Authority, European leaders refused to support Israeli calls for Arafat's replacement and continued to recognize his leadership of the Palestinians up to his death in November 2004.

If the inclusion of the PLO in the political process was a source of friction in the 1980s, Israel and Europe have been united over the question of Hamas. Following Hamas' victory in the Palestinian Parliamentary election, in January 2006, the EU conditioned all economic aid to the Palestinian Authority on Hamas accepting the Quartet principles: "non-violence, the recognition of Israel, and the acceptance of previous agreements and obligations." European governments have been steadfast in their support of president Mahmoud Abbas and in their economic and diplomatic boycott of Hamas. At the same time the EU has supported efforts aimed at reaching Palestinian reconciliation. It welcomed the March 2007 Mecca agreement leading to the formation of a Palestinian national unity government yet qualified that support by insisting that the government adopt "a platform reflecting the Quartet principles."

Since the war in Gaza at the end of 2008 an increasing number of European voices have been questioning the policy of isolating Hamas and calling for the EU to become more engaged in the process of Palestinian reconciliation.[10] Some member states, such as Ireland, Portugal and Belgium, have begun to doubt the political utility of continuing to demand the acceptance of the Quartet principles and have expressed their willingness to engage with a Palestinian government that recognizes only implicitly those conditions. While the Czech Republic and the Netherlands strongly oppose such a step, it is clear that they are in the minority. The concluding statement of the EU foreign ministers meeting of 15 June 2009 on the Middle East peace process is indicative of this trend of quietly backtracking from the Quartet principles. For the first time since Hamas took power over the Gaza Strip, the EU foreign ministers failed to call on Hamas to renounce terrorism, recognize Israel or accept previous agreements with Israel. Instead they focused on the "continued encouragement for inter-Palestinian reconciliation behind President Mahmoud Abbas and support for the mediation efforts by Egypt and the Arab League." The foreign ministers called "on all Palestinians to find common ground, based on nonviolence, in order to facilitate reconstruction in Gaza and the organisation of elections."[11]

Calls for the opening of a dialogue with Hamas have yet to result in any new policy initiative. The trend, however, is clear. Although the EU supported the Annapolis process and the negotiations between Ehud Olmert and Mahmoud Abbas, it has questioned the wisdom of a process that focuses solely on the West Bank and excludes Gaza from those discussions. Increasingly Europeans do not see the possibility of a viable resolution to the Israeli-Palestinian conflict without the inclusion of Hamas within the political process. This debate mirrors European discussions over the PLO in the late 1970s. The opening of any European dialogue with Hamas is likely to elicit a similar reaction in Israel to the European decision to formally engage with the PLO in the 1980s. As such, it creates a challenge and the need for careful mediation to prevent the potential erosion of Israeli-European relations.

For Europe, a political resolution of the Israeli-Palestinian conflict is imperative. The continuation of the conflict is seen throughout Europe as a major source of instability in the Middle East. The resolution of the Palestinian question is looked upon as a critical component in addressing Muslim unrest in the wider region and as an important element in tackling the growth of Islamic fundamentalism and international terrorism. The continuation of the Israeli-Palestinian conflict is seen as also impacting negatively on European domestic stability. Israel's occupation of the West Bank and Gaza (until 2005) and the daily images of the suffering and humiliation inflicted on the Palestinian population by Israeli policies have increasingly entered into the domestic politics of many European capitals. Europeans are determined that the Israeli-Palestinian conflict be removed as an ongoing source of international and domestic tension. Strategies that are seen as merely managing and containing the conflict, defer its resolution or prevent the emergence of a viable Palestinian state, are seen as inimical to European interests and need to be challenged. Javier Solana gave voice to Europe's frustration and determination: "Solving the Israeli-Palestinian conflict is also a fundamental European interest. Because of the impact it has on our direct neighborhood—and our own inner-cities. The only way out is the two-state solution. . . . Maintaining the status quo is not an option. We have to act now."[12]

Israeli society is deeply conflicted over the possibility of peace with the Palestinians. The majority of Israelis currently believe that the conflict cannot be resolved in the near future, and that strategies need to be adopted for its management and containment until a new Palestinian leadership arises. They regard European views on the conflict, and the chances of its immediate resolution, as flawed and illusory. European determination to affect the outcome of the Israeli-Palestinian conflict is viewed as unwarranted interference in Israeli domestic politics and as dangerous to Israeli security interests. Progress toward resolving the Israeli-Palestinian conflict has been a strong barometer, and future predictor, of the warmth of Israeli-European relations. Over the past twenty years, Israel and Europe have drawn closer together when sharing a common understanding over the strategies required and the need for negotiations aimed at ending the conflict.

Israel and Europe have not only clashed over the urgency to resolve the conflict but also over the process through which any settlement might be achieved. Europeans have not only been frustrated by their marginalization in the peace process but have often led calls for a broader role for the international community and for a greater involvement of the UN. Israel has resisted calls for an international conference to revive the peace process. It regards efforts to internationalize the peace process as an unacceptable form of pressure, and proof of Europe aligning itself with Arab positions on the conflict. Javier Solana's recent call for a UN Security Council resolution that would "proclaim the adoption of the two-state solution" and set "the parameters of borders, refugees, Jerusalem and security arrangements" has yet to be adopted by any European member state or by the EU as a whole.[13] But it is an indicator of a widely held view in Europe that the Israeli-Palestinian peace process now demands more than the resumption of negotiations under American auspices, and that additional mechanisms are required to support that process. The flouting of the idea of an internationally determined settlement, and one imposed on the parties, serves as a portent of future tensions between Israel and Europe.

Israeli-European relations have also, critically, been bound up with the transatlantic relationship. Tensions between Europe and the United States over the policies toward the Middle East, specifically the war in Iraq, the question of engaging in a diplomatic dialogue with Iran and, most notably, the Arab-Israeli peace process, have impacted negatively on Israeli-European relations. Israel sees the United States as the prime external guarantor of its long-term security. With a shared normative understanding on global issues and their extensive strategic ties, Israel has given its full support to U.S. policies in the region. In turn, it has been damning of any European objection to those policies.

In the 1980s and 1990s, successive U.S. administrations were loath to include Europe in the diplomatic efforts to resolve the Arab-Israeli conflict.

Like Israel, Washington saw European policies and actions as an impediment to peace. Throughout the Oslo process the United States kept Europe firmly on the sidelines. Since the collapse of the peace process in 2000, Europe and the United States have begun to speak increasingly with one voice on the Israeli-Palestinian conflict. The EU welcomed the issuing of the Clinton parameters in January 2001 and, as a member of the Quartet, was party to the drawing up of the 2003 Roadmap.

Today, the differences between Washington and Brussels have all but disappeared. There is a growing convergence of strategies and ideas on the Middle East, on policies toward Iraq and Iran and the resolution of the Israeli-Palestinian conflict. President Obama has been forthright in his support of Palestinian statehood. Obama's statements on Israeli settlements and his calls for a settlement freeze have been strident and uncompromising. His sense of urgency on the need for an immediate resolution to the Israeli-Palestinian conflict mirrors that of European leaders. The United States also speaks on the necessity for Palestinian reconciliation, a soft and coded message for engaging with Hamas.[14] From a European perspective, it could be argued that the United States has finally accepted its arguments and adopted its strategies on the conflict.

Without question, the United States will continue to act as the lead player in ongoing diplomatic efforts to bring the Israeli-Palestinian conflict to an end. But with its newfound commitment to multilateralism and to developing global partnerships, the EU is likely to be afforded a greater role by Washington than in the past. Increasing U.S. assertiveness toward the Israeli-Palestinian conflict might lead to a dilution of Israel's strategic partnership with the United States. This may also impact negatively on Israeli-EU relations in the short term, as Israel is forced to confront international pressures to cease its settlement activity. But, paradoxically, the convergence of U.S. and EU strategies may well remove the Palestinian issue as the central source of tension between Israel and Europe. The Israeli discourse of condemning European policies as reflective of an underlying antipathy toward Israel, in contrast to the deep-seated commitment of the United States to its security, is beginning to sound tired and anachronistic.

Israeli policies toward the conflict and EU positions and responses to those policies have impacted critically on the nature of Israeli-EU relations and on the ways that Israeli, Palestinian and European societies have viewed each other. In recent years EU policies toward Israel have comprised an uneasy mixture of incentives and soft conditionality. That ambiguity is reflected in the EU's "determination to develop a closer partnership with Israel" yet conditioning any future upgrading of Israeli-European relations on "a stronger involvement of the European Union in the peace process." As EU foreign ministers have emphasized, any future upgrade *"needs to be, and to be seen,* in the context of the broad range of our [European] common interests and objectives which notably include the resolution of the Israeli-Palestinian conflict through the implementation of the two-state solution."[15]

Since Israel's incursion into Gaza in December 2008, European states have hardened their approach. EU member states were deeply disappointed that Israel launched Operation Cast Lead within weeks of the issuing of the Brussels guidelines reaffirming the EU's commitment to the upgrading of ties.[16] European leaders and civil society were outraged by the ferocity of Israel's military response to the breakdown of the cease-fire with Hamas. The EU has condemned Israel's ongoing economic siege of Gaza, and the humanitarian suffering inflicted on the Gazan people. EU member states have become increasingly untrusting of Israel's true intentions toward the Palestinians, and have demanded that the Israeli government (re)affirm its commitment to a two-state solution to the conflict. As a consequence all discussions on the upgrade have been suspended, and the renewal of this process has become conditional on Israel taking real and effective steps toward the establishment of a viable Palestinian state. Until that point, upgrading Israel's formal standing is unlikely to feature as a high priority on the EU's agenda.

As discussed in chapter 4, both Israelis and Europeans regard Israel as part of the European family of nations yet at the same time as separate from Europe. The lack of clarity about the desired nature and the specific components of the political relationship is one of the underlying sources of tension between Israel and Europe. A new Israeli-European dialogue is required in order to detail in what ways Europe sees Israel as a future political partner. It must also address directly the status of Israel within the European family of nations and whether Israel sees itself as part of the project of the EU. Such a dialogue should begin immediately in order to prepare the groundwork for future discussions on upgrading ties.

At the political level, Israelis and Europeans need to discuss the institutional framework that will govern their future relations. In chapter 5 we presented the details of a potential new model, the "Euro-Israeli Partnership" (EIP), as a possible framework for aligning Israel with the EU below the level of full EU membership. But Israel and Europe need to move beyond a dialogue that focuses solely on technical issues and institutional frameworks to one that addresses the underlying causes and grievances that account for the difficulties in their relationship. Israelis and Europeans need to discuss not only what unites them but also what divides them. This dialogue needs to be based on an open, honest and frank exchange of ideas, aimed at developing a deeper understanding of the differences between Israel and the EU and of their divergent values. Israelis and Europeans talk of possessing a common heritage, a common set of values and shared strategic interests. There is a need to discover exactly what those shared values comprise beyond simple generalizations such as a commitment to democracy, the rule of law and the development of civil society. At the same time, Israelis and Europeans must also develop a better appreciation for how their conceptions of society, politics and national identity fundamentally differ.

This dialogue between Israel and Europe must not be driven by misperceptions, wishful thinking and false expectations. Above all, it needs to be based on a clearer recognition that Israel and the EU are fundamentally separate political projects that are located at differing stages in their historical evolution. At its most basic level, the EU comprises a post-national project wherein the member states of the EU are willing to transfer part of their sovereignty and their decision-making capacity in the realm of politics, economics, society and security to new supranational European institutions. Though nationalist sentiments are still strong at the popular level throughout the continent, European political and business elites understand the necessity of transnational cooperation on the continent even if it necessitates the foregoing of some formal attributes of sovereignty. This practical imperative is wrapped with ideological tones. Europe seeks to depict an image of having overcome its own conflictual nationalist past.

Israel and the Zionist project seek a different outcome, one more familiar with Europe's past than its present projection, namely that of state building and the creation of a state for the Jewish people. At its core, Israel is a nationalist enterprise. Sixty-one years since its establishment as a state, it is still in the process of nation-building and of creating its sense of self-identity. Loyalty is thus directed toward the institutions of the state. While many Israelis profess to be interested in and can see the long-term political and economic benefits in Israel joining the EU, the political and business elites ascribe totally to this nationalist agenda. Few Israelis would be prepared to forego elements of Israeli sovereignty to Brussels, especially if this meant any dilution of the Jewish character of the state. Although some Israeli politicians have occasionally floated the idea of Israel becoming a full member of the EU, in reality such a step is far removed from the current Israeli political agenda. Talk of this option only serves to create false expectations.

It is impossible to speak of Israeli-European relations in terms of just another set of "normal" bilateral ties. The nature of the relationship will for the foreseeable future be framed by the Jewish experience in Europe, the Holocaust and by that shared history. One cannot ignore that past, but it should not be allowed to straitjacket the discussions over future relations. Israel and Europe need to develop a greater understanding of the culture and the dynamics of each other's societies. European countries are judged by Israel through the prism of the Israeli-Palestinian conflict and by the degree of their support of Israeli positions on the conflict. Developments in Europe are refracted through Israeli concerns. Accordingly, and not surprisingly, reports of anti-Semitism receive considerable attention within the Israeli media.

The focus within the Israeli media on anti-Semitism presents a constant and painful reminder for Israelis of the Jewish experience in Europe. But this paints a distorted reality for Israelis. They hear little about political developments in Europe, of the changing dynamics within European societies, of European concerns, and of the EU's growing importance on the global stage. Absent in the current discourse is a focus on the potential opportunities for Israel in Europe and the substantive ties that have been developed. The continuing development of networks and exchanges between Israeli and European civil society (beyond the focus of the Arab-Israeli conflict) is critical to allow for a more stable foundation to Israeli-European relations.

This book opened with Dan Diner's insight that "Israel is from Europe, but not in Europe." As we have shown, Israel and Europe have drawn ever closer together. Yet Israel still lies uneasily, and will remain, at Europe's border, historically, geographically and politically. New and creative ways are needed to mediate this uneasy geopolitical relationship, as is a clearer understanding of its uniqueness and specificity. It is our hope that this book will contribute to that process.

~

Notes

Introduction

1. Statement by the European Union, "Ninth Meeting of the EU-Israel Association Council," *European Union* 15 June 2009, <http://www.delisr.ec.europa.eu/english/whatsnew.asp?id=1105> (22 July 2009).

2. Central Bureau of Statistics, *Summary of Israel's Foreign Trade by Country—2008* (Jerusalem: Central Bureau of Statistics, 2009), 1–2.

Chapter One

1. General Secretariat of the Council, "Eighth Meeting of the EU-Israel Association Council: Statement of the European Union 16 June 2008," *General Secretariat of the Council* 2008, <http://www.delisr.ec.europa.eu/english/whatsnew.asp?id=1003> (22 July 2009).

2. Council of the European Union, "Council Conclusions. Strengthening of the European Union's Bilateral Relations with its Mediterranean Partners," *Council of the European Union* 2008, <http://www.consilium.europa.eu/ueDocs/cms_Data/docs/pressdata/en/gena/104571.pdf> (22 July 2009).

3. See David Allen, "The Euro-Arab Dialogue," *Journal of Common Market Studies* 16, no. 4 (1978): 323–42; and Haiifaa A. Jawad, *Euro-Arab Relations: A Study in Collective Diplomacy* (Reading: Ithaca Press, 1992).

4. Quoted in Ilan Greilsammer and Joseph H.H. Weiler, "European Political Cooperation and the Palestinian-Israeli Conflict: An Israeli Perspective," in *European Foreign Policy Making and the Arab-Israeli Conflict*, ed. David Allen and Alfred Pijpers (London: Pinter, 1984), 136.

5. For text of the Venice declaration see, <http://www.knesset.gov.il/process/docs/venice_eng.htm> (29 July 2009).

6. <http://www.mfa.gov.il> (29 July 2009).

7. Shimon Peres, *The New Middle East* (New York: Henry Holt & Co, 1993).

8. Council of the European Union, "European Council Meeting on 9 and 10 December 1994 in Essen. Presidency Conclusions," *Council of the European Union* 1994, <http://www.consilium.europa.eu/ueDocs/cms_Data/docs/pressData/en/ec/003001 .EN4.htm> (25 July 2009).

9. For an in-depth discussion of the 1995 Association Agreement see chapter 3.

10. Rosemary Hollis, "Europe and the Middle East: Power By Stealth?" *International Affairs* 73, no. 1 (1997): 15–29.

11. Council of the European Union, "Presidency Conclusions. Berlin European Council 24 and 25 March 1999," *Council of the European Union* 1999, <http://www.consilium.europa.eu/ueDocs/cms_Data/docs/pressData/en/ec/ACFB2.html> (27 July 2009). See discussion below.

12. European Commission, "Jerusalem and Ramallah Heads of Mission Report on East Jerusalem," *European Commission* 2005, <http://www.fhfpal.org/mis/eu_report .htm> (29 July 2009).

13. Quoted in Hollis, "Europe and the Middle East," 23.

14. Chirac was involved in a public scuffle with Israeli security guards while touring the Old City, resulting in Israel issuing a public apology to the French president. He also addressed the Palestinian Legislative Council in Ramallah during his visit to the region, becoming the first head of state to do so.

15. *Jerusalem Post*, 5 November 1996.

16. European Commission, "The EU Action Strategy for Peace in the Middle East: The Way Forward," *European Commission*, (November 2008): 3.

17. The massacre took place on 9 April 1948, when fighters from the Jewish Zionist undergrounds attacked the Palestinian-Arab village of Deir Yassin near Jerusalem. Around 107 Arabs were killed during the attack which was meant to relieve the blockade of Jerusalem.

18. Council of the European Union, "Cardiff European Council 15 and 16 June 1998. Presidency Conclusions," *Council of the European Union* 1998, <http://www .consilium.europa.eu/ueDocs/cms_Data/docs/pressData/en/ec/54315.pdf> (25 July 2009).

19. Council of the European Union, "Berlin European Council."

20. *Jerusalem Post*, 26 March 1999.

21. Council of the European Union, "Seville European Council 21 and 22 June 2002. Presidency Conclusions," *Council of the European Union* 2002, <http://www .consilium.europa.eu/ueDocs/cms_Data/docs/pressData/en/ec/72638.pdf> (29 July 2009).

22. "Legal Consequences of the Construction of a Wall in the Occupied Palestinian Territory, Advisory Opinion," *I.C.J. Reports* 2004, <http://www.icj-cij.org/docket/files/131/1671.pdf> (29 July 2009).

23. Israeli Ministry of Foreign Affairs, "Israel: UN Vote Encourages Palestinian Terrorism," *Israeli Ministry of Foreign Affairs* 2004, <http://www.mfa.gov.il> (29 July 2009).

24. Shlomo Shamir, "FM: EU Vote Encourages PA to Avoid Fighting Terror," *Haaretz*, 22 July 2004.

25. Reuters, "Israel Pledges Major Investment in EU's Galileo Project," *Haaretz*, 13 July 2004.

26. "French Jews Must Move to Israel," *BBC News*, 18 July 2004.

27. Gerald M. Steinberg, "Learning the Lessons of the European Union's Failed Middle East Policies," *Jerusalem Viewpoints* 510, (2004).

28. Declaration of the European Union, "Fourth Meeting of the Association Council EU-Israel," *European Union* 17–18 November 2003, <http://www.consilium.europa.eu/ueDocs/cms_Data/docs/pressData/en/er/77932.pdf> (22 July 2009). The EU was "particularly concerned by the route marked out for the so-called security fence in the Occupied West Bank and East Jerusalem. The envisaged departure of the route from the 'green line' could prejudge future negotiations and make the two-state solution physically impossible to implement."

29. Reuters, "EU's Solana Shocked at Israeli Settlement Growth," *Haaretz*, 22 January 2007.

30. Barak Ravid, "Britain Steps Up Fight against West Bank Settlements," *Haaretz*, 18 December 2008. For an in-depth discussion of "the rules of origin dispute" see chapter 3.

31. Declaration of the European Union, "Third Meeting of the Association Council EU-Israel," *European Union* 21 October 2002, <http://www.consilium.europa.eu/ueDocs/cms_Data/docs/pressData/en/er/72832.pdf> (29 July 2009).

32. Ian Black, Ewan MacAskill and Nicholas Watt, "Israel Faces Rage Over 'Massacre,'" *The Guardian*, 17 April 2002.

33. Flash Eurobarometer, *Iraq and Peace in the World—Full Report 151*, *European Commission* 2003, <http://www.mafhoum.com/press6/167P52.pdf> (29 July 2009).

34. Suzanne Gershowitz and Emanuele Ottolenghi, "Europe's Problem with Ariel Sharon," *Middle East Quarterly* 2005, <http://www.meforum.org/743/europes-problem-with-ariel-sharon> (29 July 2009).

35. Council of the European Union, "Seville European Council."

36. Council of the European Union, "Brussels European Council 25 and 26 March 2004. Presidency Conclusions," *Council of the European Union* 2004, <http://consilium.europa.eu/ueDocs/cms_Data/docs/pressData/en/ec/79696.pdf> (29 July 2009).

37. For further information about EUBAM Rafah visit the mission's website at <http://www.eubam-rafah.eu/portal> (29 July 2009).

38. Council of the European Union, "Summary of Remarks to the Press by Javier Solana EU High Representative for the CFSP on the Gaza Crisis," *Council of the European Union* 2009, <http://www.consilium.europa.eu/ueDocs/cms_Data/docs/pressdata/EN/discours/105460.pdf> (29 July 2009).

39. In a related development, UN Security Council Resolution 1701 of August ended 34 days of a war between Israel and Hezbollah in Lebanon. The Resolution strengthened UNIFIL's (United Nations Interim Force in Lebanon) mandate and increased the number of UNIFIL troops in southern Lebanon from 2,000 to 15,000 (UNIFIL II). EU member states have provided more than 7,000 soldiers to UNIFIL II. Although UNIFIL II is not an EU operation, the European participation in the mission is the backbone of this new force. For the first time, the EU plays a central and crucial role as a single entity in the Israeli-Lebanese/Hezbollah conflict.

40. See Christian-Peter Hanelt, "After Annapolis: What is the European Role in Facilitating the Implementation of a Two-State Solution?" in *Bound to Cooperate II – Europe and the Middle East*, ed. Christian-Peter Hanelt and Almut Möller (Gütersloh: Verlag Bertelsmann Stiftung, 2008), 214.

41. Jarat Chopra, "Third Party Monitoring in the Israeli-Palestinian Conflict," *The International Spectator* 38, no. 4 (2003): 33–45.

42. See Clara Marina O'Donnell, "The EU, Israel and Hamas," *Centre for European Reform Working Paper* 2008, <http://www.cer.org.uk/pdf/wp_820.pdf> (29 July 2009); Clara Marina O'Donnell, "The EU's Approach to Israel and the Palestinians: A Move in the Right Direction," *Centre for European Reform Policy Brief* 2009, <http://www.cer.org.uk/pdf/pb_israel_18june09.pdf> (29 July 2009).

43. General Secretariat of the Council, "Eighth Meeting of the EU-Israel Association Council: Statement of the European Union 16 June 2008," *General Secretariat of the Council* 2008, <http://www.delisr.ec.europa.eu/english/whatsnew.asp?id=1003> (22 July 2009).

44. For an in-depth discussion of the upgrade process of Israeli-EU relations see chapter 3.

Chapter Two

1. For a detailed analysis of the Regional Economic Development Working Group (REDWG) see Joel Peters, *Pathways to Peace: The Multilateral Arab-Israeli Peace Talks* (London: Royal Institute of International Affairs, 1996), 46–60.

2. The areas covered were: communications and transport (led by France); energy (EU); tourism (Japan); agriculture (Spain); financial markets (UK); trade (Germany); training (United States); networks (EU); institutions, sectors and principles (Egypt); and bibliography (Canada).

3. See Dalia Dassa Kaye, "Banking on Peace: Lessons from the Middle East Development Bank," *Institute on Global Conflict and Cooperation (IGCC) Policy Papers* 1998, <http://repositories.cdlib.org/igcc/PP/pp43> (10 July 2009).

4. Alfred Tovias, "Israel and the Barcelona Process," *EuroMeSCo Working Papers* 1998, <http://www.euromesco.net/euromesco/index.php?option=com_content&task =view&id=135&Itemid=48&lang=en> (10 July 2009).

5. David Ohana, "Israel Towards a Mediterranean Identity," in *Integration and Identity Challenges to Europe and Israel*, ed. Shlomo Avineri and Werner Weidenfeld (Bonn: Europa Union Verlag, 1999), 84–99.

6. For an excellent discussion of Israeli identity and the Mediterranean see Raffaella A. Del Sarto, "Region-Building, European Union Normative Power and Contested Identities: The Case of Israel," in *The Convergence of Civilizations: Constructing a Mediterranean Region*, ed. Emanuel Adler, Federica Bicchi, Beverly Crawford and Raffaella A. Del Sarto (Toronto: University of Toronto Press, 2006) 296–333; see also Raffaella A. Del Sarto, *Contested State Identities and Regional Security in the Euro-Mediterranean Area* (Houndmills: Palgrave Macmillan, 2006), 87–129.

7. *Middle East International*, 18 April 1997.

8. General Affairs Council, "Declaration by the European Union on the Middle East Peace Process," *General Affairs Council* 1 October 1996, <http://www.unispal.un.org/.../0e16f7f1d4d58ab2852563bd0054e424?> (20 July 2009).

9. Tovias, "Israel and Barcelona Process."

10. European Commission, "Statement by the European Commission on the Role of the European Union in the Middle East Peace Process," *European Commission* 16 January 1998, <http://unispal.un.org/unispal.nsf/d80185e9f0c69a7b85256cbf005afea c/ce71a61cbb81e7bf85256e370056c8ef?OpenDocument> (10 July 2009).

11. EuroMeSCo, "EuroMeSCo Joint Report: Working Group on Political and Security Cooperation and Working Group on Arms Control, Confidence Building and Conflict Prevention," *EuroMeSCo Joint Reports* (April 1997).

12. Fred Tanner, "The Euro-Med Partnership: Prospects for Arms Limitations and Confidence Building After Malta," *The International Spectator* 32, no. 2 (1997): 3–25.

13. European Commission, *The Barcelona Process. Five Years On (1995–2000)* (Luxembourg: Office for Official Publications of the European Communities, 2000).

14. Fathy El Shazly, "The Development of the Euro-Mediterranean Charter for Peace and Stability," in *The Future of the Euro-Mediterranean Security Dialogue*, ed. Martin Ortega (Paris: The Institute for Security Studies Western European Union Occasional Papers, 2000), 27.

15. Euro-Mediterranean Partnership, "Presidency Formal Conclusions. Fourth Euro-Mediterranean Conference of Foreign Ministers, Marseilles 15–16 November 2000," *Euro-Mediterranean Partnership* 2000, <http://www.medea.be/index .html?page=2&lang=en&doc> (20 July 2009).

16. Euro-Mediterranean Partnership, "Valencia Action Plan, Fifth Euro-Mediterranean Conference of Foreign Ministers, Valencia 22–23 April 2002," *Euro-Mediterranean Partnership* 2002, <http://www.ces.es/TRESMED/docum/Conf_2002_Valencia_ en.pdf> (20 July 2009).

17. French Presidency of the EU Council, "Joint Declaration of the Paris Summit for the Mediterranean, Paris 13 July 2008," *French Presidency of the EU Council 2008*,

<http://www.eu2008.fr/webdav/site/PFUE/shared/import/07/0713_declaration_de_
paris/Joint_declaration_of_the_Paris_summit_for_the_Mediterranean-EN.pdf> (17
May 2009).

18. Michael R. Sesit, "Sarkozy's Club Med Experiment Is Sure to Fail," *Bloomberg
.com* 2008, <http://www.bloomberg.com/apps/news?sid=alBeLe8eQpl4&pid=20601
039> (31 July 2008).

19. French Presidency of the EU Council, "Final Statement: Marseille 3–4
November 2008," *French Presidency of the EU Council* 2008, <http://www.eu2008
.fr/webdav/site/PFUE/shared/import/1103_ministerielle_Euromed/Final_Statement_
Mediterranean_Union_EN.pdf> (17 May 2009).

20. The UfM uses a very broad definition for the "Mediterranean area" which
includes some non-Mediterranean littoral states and entities.

21. While the Arab League is a member of the UfM and is allowed to participate
in all its meetings at all levels, it has no voting rights in the UfM.

22. The UfM comprises six areas of action: (i) the first area includes projects such
as interconnection of Mediterranean ports, upgrading of technical and logistical
capabilities, and auto-routes connection; (ii) the second area includes projects such
as waste water management, desalination, protection of the marine environment,
preservation of natural resources and wealth of the deep sea, and integrated Mediterranean water strategy; (iii) the third UfM area includes projects such as Mediterranean solar plan, and interconnection of electric power transmission grids among the
countries and regions that encircle the Mediterranean Sea ("Mediterranean Ring");
(iv) the fourth area includes projects such as interoperable information system, and
coordinated prevention, warning and disaster management systems; (v) the fifth
area includes projects such as Mediterranean university, Mediterranean center for
research, and vocational trainings; (vi) the last area includes projects such as integrated projects to foster cooperation between the business community, and projects
to assist small and medium-sized enterprises.

23. See discussion in chapter 3.

24. Dimitar Bechev and Kalypso Nicolaidis, "The Union for the Mediterranean:
A Genuine Breakthrough or More of the Same?" *The International Spectator* 43, no.
3 (2008): 13–20.

25. "Interview with an Israeli Senior Official," Jerusalem, 5 February 2007.

26. Katrin Bennhold, "Sarkozy's Proposal for Mediterranean Bloc Makes Waves,"
International Herald Tribune 10 May 2007, <http://www.nytimes.com/2007/05/10/
world/europe/10iht-france.4.5656114.html?_r=1> (28 May 2009).

27. Ehud Olmert, "Speech by Prime Minister Ehud Olmert's to the Mediterranean Union Summit," *Israel Prime Minister's Office* 2008, <http://www.pmo.gov
.il/NR/rdonlyres/1E56BE9B-257E-4E66-B34E-FB3D7A0DA009/0/parisENG130708
.doc> (28 May 2009).

28. Eran Lerman, *The Mediterranean Idea: Envisioning a Brighter Future for All the
Peoples of the Mediterranean* (Jerusalem: American Jewish Committee, 2007), 2. See

also Uri Savir, "Pax Mediterraneo," *Israel Journal of Foreign Affairs* 3, no. 1 (2009): 55–61.

Chapter Three

1. European Communities, "Euro-Mediterranean Agreement Establishing an Association between the European Communities and their Member States, of the One Part, and the State of Israel, of the Other Part," *Official Journal of the European Communities* 2000/L 147/3 2000, <http://www.delisr.ec.europa.eu/english/content/eu_and_country/asso_agree_en.pdf> (20 July 2009).

2. Mixed agreements are of enormous legal significance for the international relations of the Union. They are used in different circumstances and dominate in the Treaty practice of the EC; Dominic McGoldrick, *International Relations Law of the European Union* (Essex: Longman, 1997), 78–88.

3. <http://www.mfa.gov.il> (20 July 2009).

4. Peter Malanczuk, "The Legal Framework of the Economic Relations between Israel and the European Union," in *Israel Among the Nations*, ed. Alfred E. Kellermann, Kurt Siehr and Talia Einhorn (Leiden: Brill Academic Publishers, 1999), 263–79.

5. EU-Israel Association Agreement: Articles 6–28 and Protocol Four concerning the definition of the concept "originating products" and methods of administrative cooperation.

6. Once adopted, the agreement created new opportunities for Israeli and EU exporters in a large range of products that could not previously reach Israeli and European markets.

7. EU-Israel Association Agreement: Articles 29, 31–4, 64–6.

8. Lior Herman, "An Action Plan or a Plan for Action? Israel and the European Neighbourhood Policy," *Mediterranean Politics* 11, no. 3 (2006): 371–94.

9. EU-Israel Association Agreement: Articles 41–57.

10. EU-Israel Association Agreement: Articles 63–6.

11. EU-Israel Association Agreement: Articles 58–61.

12. Government of Israel, "Cabinet Decision on Free Trade Treaty with the European Union. Resolution Number 57, 7 June 1995," *Government Resolutions* 15, (1995–1996, June 1995).

13. EU-Israel Association Agreement: Articles 3–5, 67, 70–5. On 13 June 2000, the Association Council held its first meeting in Luxembourg, headed by Israel's foreign minister David Levy and the foreign ministers of the EU member states, marking the entry into force of the Association Agreement.

14. For a discussion of Israel's lack of grand strategy toward the EU see Yehezkel Dror and Sharon Pardo, "Approaches and Principles for an Israeli Grand-Strategy towards the European Union," *European Foreign Affairs Review* 11, no. 1 (2006): 17–44.

15. The "Europe Agreements" formed the legal bases for association between CEEC and the EU enabling CEEC to gradually integrate into the EU. Europe Agreements mostly covered the establishment of free trade areas, liberalization of economic activity, technical and legal assistance, participation in Union's programs, and political dialogues. See Neill Nugent, "The Unfolding of the 10 + 2 Enlargement Round," in *European Union Enlargement*, ed. Neill Nugent (Basingstoke and New York: Palgrave Macmillan, 2004), 34–55.

16. The so-called "EUR 1 form" which is used in multilateral agreements within the Pan-European preference system. The exporter fills out the EUR 1 form and then sends it to the customs authority, which approves the form, stamps it and returns it to the exporter.

17. European Commission, "Notice to Importers: Importations from Israel into the Community," *Official Journal of the European Communities* 1997/C 338/13, (8 November 1997).

18. Under the Barcelona Process, a system of Pan-Euro-Mediterranean cumulation of origin was created. For this purpose on 11 October 2005, the EU Council approved a Commission proposal to amend protocols on rules of origin annexed to the various Association Agreements. The system will be applicable between the Union and Algeria, Egypt, Israel, Jordan, Lebanon, Morocco, Syria, Tunisia, West Bank and Gaza Strip, the EEA/EFTA countries, the Faroe Islands and Turkey.

19. Convention (IV) relative to the Protection of Civilian Persons in Time of War. Geneva, 12 August 1949. Article 1 of the Convention provides that the "High Contracting Parties undertake to respect and to ensure respect for the present Convention in all circumstances."

20. European Commission, "Communication from the Commission to the Council and the European Parliament. Implementations of the Interim Agreement on Trade and Trade Related Matters between the European Community and Israel, SEC(1998) 695 final," *European Commission*, (12 May 1998).

21. In the early 1980s Israel unilaterally annexed East Jerusalem and the Golan Heights. Article 1 of the Basic Law: Jerusalem, Capital of Israel, 30 July 1980, declares that "Jerusalem, complete and united, is the capital of Israel." Article 1 of the Golan Heights Law, 14 December 1981, provides that "The law, jurisdiction and administration of the state shall apply to the Golan Heights, as described in the Appendix."

22. Quoted in Wybe Th. Douma, "Israel and the Palestinian Authority," in *The European Union and Its Neighbours: A Legal Appraisal of the EU's Policies of Stabilisation, Partnership and Integration*, ed. Steven Blockmans and Adam Lazowski (The Hague: T.M.C Asser Press, 2006), 447.

23. European Commission, "Notice to Importers: Imports from Israel into the Community," *Official Journal of the European Communities* 2001/C 328/04, (23 November 2001).

24. In December 2005, with the conclusion of this dispute, the Council of Ministers amended the Protocol providing for Israel's inclusion in the system of cumulation.

25. For example: "Israel, Kedumim, D.N. Shomron 44856" (Kedumim is an Israeli settlement in the West Bank).

26. European Commission, "Communication from the Commission to the Council and the European Parliament: Wider Europe—Neighbourhood: A New Framework for Relations with our Eastern and Southern Neighbours, COM(2003) 104 final," *European Commission* 11 March 2003, <http://ec.europa.eu/world/enp/pdf/com03_104_en.pdf> (20 July 2009).

27. Raffaella A. Del Sarto and Tobias Schumacher, "From EMP to ENP: What's at Stake with the European Neighbourhood Policy towards the Southern Mediterranean?" *European Foreign Affairs Review* 10, no. 1 (2005): 22.

28. Romano Prodi, "A Wider Europe—A Proximity Policy as the Key to Stability. 'Peace, Security and Stability International Dialogue and the Role of the EU.' Sixth ECSA—World Conference, SPEECH/02/619," *European Commission*, (6 December 2009).

29. Silvan Shalom, "Address by Israeli Foreign Minister Silvan Shalom to the European Union Council of Ministers," *Israeli Ministry of Foreign Affairs*, (21 July 2003).

30. Adar Primor, "The Leading Star of Wider Europe," *Haaretz*, 21 July 2003.

31. David Kriss, "Commissioner Verheugen: Israel a 'Natural Partner for EU' in New Neighbourhood Policy," *Europe in Israel Newsletter*, July 2003.

32. EU-Israel Association Council, "EU/Israel Action Plan," *EU-Israel Association Council* 2004, <http://ec.europa.eu/world/enp/pdf/action_plans/israel_enp_ap_final_en.pdf> (21 July 2009). The Action Plan was adopted for a period of three years, which was extended for another year and expired in April 2009. On 15 June 2009, the EU proposed to Israel that the Action Plan remain the reference document for Israeli-EU relations until a new instrument is adopted. In August 2009 Israel and the EU agreed to extend the Action Plan until 31 December 2009.

33. David Kriss, "European Neighbourhood Policy: Israel Action Plan Endorsed," *Europe in Israel Newsletter*, February 2005.

34. Kriss, "European Neighborhood Policy," 2.

35. Herb Keinon, "Israel Okays Wider Europe Action Plan," *The Jerusalem Post*, 15 December 2004.

36. EU-Israel Action Plan.

37. European Commission, "Israel Joins EU Competitiveness Programme," *Europa Press Release Rapid* 2007, <http://europa.eu/rapid/pressReleasesAction.do?reference=IP/07/1643&format=HTML&aged=1&language=EN&guiLanguage=en> (20 July 2009). CIP supports innovation activities, provides better access to finance and delivers business support services. CIP encourages a better take-up and use of information and communications technologies and helps to develop the information society. CIP also promotes the increased use of renewable energies and energy efficiency. Israel already joined the first pillar "Entrepreneurship and Innovation" under the CIP program. This pillar fosters the competitiveness of enterprises, and links providers of business and innovation services into a European network, as

well as linking innovation actors and clusters in European networks. Through the CIP, Israel can cooperate with all EU member states and with other third countries joining the CIP, on a whole host of projects on competitiveness and innovation. The CIP program runs from 2007 to 2013 with a budget of €3.6 billion.

38. European Commission, "Communication from the Commission to the Council and the European Parliament 'Implementation of the European Neighbourhood Policy in 2007' Progress Report Israel, Brussels, SEC(2008) 394," *European Commission* 3 April 2008, <http://ec.europa.eu/world/enp/pdf/progress2008/sec08_394_en.pdf> (20 July 2009).

39. Shalom, "Address by Israeli Foreign Minister."

40. Shlomo Shamir, "FM: EU Vote Encourages PA to Avoid Fighting Terror," *Haaretz*, 22 July 2004.

41. For a discussion of the economic aspects of the Action Plan see Herman, "An Action Plan or a Plan for Action?"

42. For an excellent discussion see Raffaella A. Del Sarto, "Wording and Meaning(s): EU-Israeli Political Cooperation according to the ENP Action Plan," *Mediterranean Politics* 11, no. 1 (2007): 59–74.

43. Del Sarto, "Wording and Meaning(s)," 62.

44. European Commission, "Progress Report on the Implementation of the European Neighbourhood Policy, SEC(2008) 394, *European Commission* 3 April 2008, <http://ec.europa.eu/world/enp/documents_en.htm#3> (26 July 2009).

45. The Action Plan provides that Israel and the EU will "promote co-operation in the field of cultural and linguistic heritage, including, where possible, protection of minority languages (e.g., Yiddish and Ladino)."

46. Shmuel Trigano, "The European Neighbourhood Policy and the European Jewish Communities," (paper presented at the joint seminar of the Israeli Association for the Study of European Integration and the Jewish People Policy Planning Institute, Jerusalem, March 2006).

47. "Israel and the EU Endorsed a New Agreement," *The Jerusalem Post*, 13 December 2004.

48. "Barcelona Declaration on Euro-Mediterranean Partnership," 1995, <http://europa.eu/legislation_summaries/external_relations/relations_with_third_countries/mediterranean_partner_countries/r15001_en.htm> (28 July 2009).

49. Tzipi Livni, "Israel and the European Union in the Enlarged Neighbourhood," *Europe in BGU Newsletter*, March 2007, 1–4.

50. General Secretariat of the Council, "Eighth Meeting of the EU-Israel Association Council: Statement of the European Union 16 June 2008," *General Secretariat of the Council* 2008, <http://www.delisr.ec.europa.eu/english/whatsnew.asp?id=1003> (22 July 2009).

51. Council of the European Union, "Council Conclusions. Strengthening of the European Union's Bilateral Relations with its Mediterranean Partners," *Council of the European Union* 2008, <http://www.consilium.europa.eu/ueDocs/cms_Data/docs/pressdata/en/gena/104571.pdf> (22 July 2009).

52. Benita Ferrero-Waldner, "The Offer on the Table," *Haaretz*, 17 April 2009.

53. See Barak Ravid, "Israel to EU: Criticism of Netanyahu Government Unacceptable," *Haaretz*, 30 April 2009; and Akiva Eldar, "Livni Urges EU: Don't Halt EU-Israel Relations Upgrade," *Haaretz*, 24 April 2004.

54. Statement by the European Union, "Ninth Meeting of the EU-Israel Association Council," *European Union* 15 June 2009, <http://www.delisr.ec.europa .eu/english/whatsnew.asp?id=1105> (22 July 2009).

Chapter Four

1. Tzipi Livni, "Israel and the European Union in the Enlarged Neighbourhood," *Europe in BGU Newsletter*, March 2007, 1–4.

2. The information for the tables in this chapter is compiled from research carried out in 2008 by Sharon Pardo, with the assistance of Michal Eskenazi and Ayal Kantz, at the Centre for the Study of European Politics and Society, Ben-Gurion University of the Negev, Israel.

3. Konrad-Adenauer-Stiftung and Sharon Pardo, *Measuring the Attitudes of Israelis towards the European Union and its Member States* (Jerusalem: Konrad-Adenauer-Stiftung, 2007); Konrad-Adenauer-Stiftung and Sharon Pardo, *Measuring the Attitudes of Israelis towards the European Union and its Member States* (Jerusalem: Konrad-Adenauer-Stiftung, 2009). The KAS and Pardo 2007 survey was carried out in February 2007, by Keevoon Research, Strategy & Communications. A representative sample of 511 people responded to the survey with a margin of error of 4.5 percent. The KAS and Pardo 2009 survey was carried out in April 2009, also by Keevoon Research, Strategy & Communications, and included 600 people with a margin of error of 4.1 percent.

4. The Dahaf 2004 survey was commissioned by the European Commission's Delegation to Israel and was conducted by the Dahaf Institute in December 2003 and in February 2004. A representative sample of 997 people responded to the survey.

5. Konrad-Adenauer-Stiftung and Pardo, *Measuring the Attitudes* (2009), 26–9, 56.

6. Dahaf Institute, *Israelis' Attitudes Towards the European Union* (Tel Aviv: Dahaf Institute, 2004), 24.

7. Konrad-Adenauer-Stiftung and Pardo, *Measuring the Attitudes* (2007), 17.

8. In addition 64 percent of Israelis thought that the EU is not doing enough to prevent Islamophobia; Konrad-Adenauer-Stiftung and Pardo, *Measuring the Attitudes* (2007), 18–19.

9. Dahaf, *Israelis' Attitudes*, 41.

10. Transnational Radical Party, "For Israel in the EU," *Transnational Radical Party* 2002, <http://servizi.radicalparty.org/israel_ue/appeal/english.php> (7 August 2009).

11. "Israel Should Join the European Union," *Galatz-IDF Radio*, 9 November 2002.

12. "Analysis: Israel Weighing EU Membership," *United Press International*, 21 May 2003.

13. "Liberman: Israel Should Press to Join NATO, EU," *Haaretz*, 1 January 2007.

14. Yisrael Beytenu, "Yisrael Beytenu's Vision," *Yisrael Beytenu* 2009, <http://bey tenu.org./107/1172/article.html> (7 August 2009).

15. "EU Membership Touted for Israel, Palestine, Jordan," *CBC News*, 11 February 2004.

16. "Berlusconi: Italy will Support Israeli EU Membership," *Globes*, 3 October 2004.

17. "Statements by PM Olmert and European leaders," *Ynet*, 18 January 2009. Berlusconi made the statement at a joint news conference with four other European leaders who arrived in Israel to support the Israeli-Hamas cease-fire.

18. Nicolas Sarkozy, *Testimony* (New York: Pantheon Books, 2007), 148.

19. Transnational Radical Party, "For Israel in the EU." It is interesting to note that the Austrian far-right party One Freedom (FPÖ) advocates the opposite view and fights against Israeli membership in the EU. In its June 2009 European Parliament election campaign, FPÖ promised to veto the EU membership of Israel and Turkey in order to avoid getting involved in what the party described as "the bloody Middle East crisis"; "Far-Right Party Throws Austrian Politics into Turmoil ahead of EU Elections," *Deutsche Welle*, 1 June 2009.

20. "SPD-Politiker wünscht sich Israel als EU-Mitglied," *Hamburger Abendblatt*, 4 June 2009.

21. Itamar Eichner, "An Advocacy Lesson: At a Jerusalem Conference Sharon Demanded from Israel's Ambassadors to Europe: Do Not Be Afraid of Anyone," *Yedioth Ahronoth*, 29 December 2004.

22. "Olmert in a Rare Statement: Rice Remained Ashamed of Herself," *Ynet*, 12 January 2009.

23. "Netanyahu: Europe Will Not Dictate Terms to Us, Peace is also in Israel's Interest," *Haaretz*, 24 April 2009.

24. "European Report on Anti-Semitism Shelved Due to 'Political' Reasons," *Israelinsider*, 24 November 2003.

25. "Sharon: Antisemitism in Europe has Reached New Levels after the Holocaust," *Ynet*, 27 January 2004.

26. "French Jews Must Move to Israel," *BBC News*, 18 July 2004.

27. Tzipi Livni, "Address to the Global Forum for Combating Anti-Semitism," *Israel Ministry of Foreign Affairs* (11 February 2009).

28. Council of the European Union, "Council Conclusions. Strengthening of the European Union's Bilateral Relations with its Mediterranean Partners," *Council of the European Union* 2008, <http://www.consilium.europa.eu/ueDocs/cms_Data/docs/pressdata/en/gena/104571.pdf> (22 July 2009).

29. This section draws upon Yehezkel Dror and Sharon Pardo, "Approaches and Principles for an Israeli Grand Strategy towards the European Union," *European Foreign Affairs Review* 11, no. 3 (2006): 17–44.

30. The Law of Return 5710-1950 stipulates that Jews immigrating to Israel may be granted the status of *Oleh*, which automatically entitles them to citizenship, unless the applicant is deemed likely to endanger public health, the security of the state or public welfare, and so on.

31. Adar Primor, "EU Commissioner for External Relations: We will Take Advantage of the Improvement of Relations with the U.S. for a Deeper Involvement of the EU in the Peace Process," *Haaretz*, 8 February 2005.

32. Council of the European Union, "A Secure Europe in a Better World: European Security Strategy," *European Council* 12 December 2003, <http://www.con silium.europa.eu/uedocs/cmsUpload/78367.pdf> (10 July 2009).

33. Council of the European Union, "A Secure Europe," 8.

34. Council of the European Union, "A Secure Europe," 14.

35. "Italian FM: EU Biased Against Israel," *Haaretz*, 19 June 2008.

36. "Interview with the Director General of One of the Largest Israeli Civil Society Organizations," *Jerusalem*, 24 January 2008.

37. *Haaretz* is commonly referred to as "a newspaper for thinking people," *Yedioth Ahronoth* is known as "the nation's newspaper" and *Maariv* is known as "everybody's newspaper."

38. Konrad-Adenauer-Stiftung and Pardo, *Measuring the Attitudes* (2009), 45.

39. Mark Leonard, *Why Europe Will Run the 21st Century* (New York: PublicAffairs, 2005), 49–56.

40. Francois Duchêne, "Israel in the Eyes of the Europeans: A Speculative Essay," in *Europe and Israel: Troubled Neighbors*, ed. Ilan Greilsammer and Joseph Weiler (New York: Walter de Gruyter, 1980), 11.

Chapter Five

1. Council of the European Union, "Council Conclusions. Strengthening of the European Union's Bilateral Relations with its Mediterranean Partners," *Council of the European Union* 2008, <http://www.consilium.europa.eu/ueDocs/cms_Data/docs/pressdata/en/gena/104571.pdf> (22 July 2009).

2. Benita Ferrero-Waldner, "Bilateral Relations Between Israel and the European Union," *European Commission*, (27 September 2007). For a discussion on principles underlying a future Israeli strategy toward the EU, see Yehezkel Dror and Sharon Pardo, "Approaches and Principles for an Israeli Grand Strategy towards the European Union," *European Foreign Affairs Review* 11, no.1 (2006): 17–44.

3. David Phinnemore, *Association: Stepping-Stone or Alternative to EU Membership* (Sheffield: Sheffield Academic Press, 1999), 23.

4. "'Close Relations' More Fashionable than Enlargement," *EurActiv.com*, 10 July 2008.

5. Parliament of the European Union, "European Parliament Resolution of 10 July on the Commission's 2007 Enlargement Strategy Paper, (2007/2271(INI))," *Parliament of the European Union*, (10 July 2008): paragraphs 18–20.

6. Court of Justice of the European Communities, *Case 12/86, Meryem Demirel v. Stadt Schwäbisch Gmünd*, ECR 1987: 3719-55. The case involved a Turkish woman who came to Germany and was ordered to leave the country when her visa expired. The ECJ ruled that, at that time, the rights to family reunification were not covered by the EC-Turkey Association Agreement. In its ruling the ECJ observed that the Community may conclude "an agreement creating special, privileged links with a non-member country." While the ECJ refrained from any elaboration on the substance of these "privileged links" with the non-member country, the Court's statement suggests that the relations should be based on more than just a regular trade agreement; Paul Craig and Gráinne De Búrca, *EU Law: Text, Cases and Materials* (Oxford: Oxford University Press, 2003), 343.

7. Phinnemore, *Association*.

8. The following sections draw on Thérèse Blanchet, Risto Piipponen and Maria Westman-Clément, *The Agreement on the European Economic Area (EEA): A Guide to the Free Movement of Goods and Competition Rules* (Oxford: Clarendon Press, 1994).

9. The committee system that EU member states established to oversee the execution of EU policies.

10. Court of Justice of the European Communities, *Opinion 1/91 of Dec. 1991*, ECR I-6079.

11. José Manuel Barroso, "Shared Challenges, Shared Futures: Taking the Neighbourhood Policy Forward," *European Commission*, (3 September 2007).

12. European Commission, "European Commission Communication from the Commission: A Strong European Neighbourhood Policy, COM(2007) 774 final," *European Commission* 5 December 2007, <http://www.ec.europa.eu/world/enp/pdf/com07_774_en.pdf> (10 July 2009).

13. "Israel Should Join the European Union," *Galatz-IDF Radio*, 9 November 2002.

14. "Liberman: Israel Should Press to Join NATO, EU," *Haaretz*, 1 January 2007.

15. Yisrael Beytenu, "Yisrael Beytenu's Vision," *Yisrael Beytenu* 2009, <http://beytenu.org./107/1172/article.html> (7 Aug. 2009).

16. "Proceedings of the 2nd Annual KAS-BGU Round on Israeli-EU Relations," Jerusalem, 1 May 2007.

17. Konrad-Adenauer-Stiftung and Sharon Pardo, *Measuring the Attitudes of Israelis towards the European Union and its Member States* (Jerusalem: Konrad-Adenauer-Stiftung, 2009), 26–9. See also chapter 4, table 4.3.

18. Romano Prodi, "A Wider Europe—A Proximity Policy as the Key to Stability. 'Peace, Security and Stability International Dialogue and the Role of the EU.' Sixth ECSA—World Conference, SPEECH/02/619," *European Commission*, (6 December 2009).

19. Tzipi Livni, "Israel and the European Union in the Enlarged Neighbourhood," *Europe in BGU Newsletter*, March 2007, 1–4.

Conclusion

1. Central Bureau of Statistics, *Summary of Israel's Foreign Trade by Country—2008* (Jerusalem: Central Bureau of Statistics, 2009), 1–2; Statement by the European Union, "Ninth Meeting of the EU-Israel Association Council," *European Union* 15 June 2009, <http://www.delisr.ec.europa.eu/English/whatsnew.asp?id=1105> (22 July 2009).

2. Statement by the European Union, "Ninth Meeting."

3. Israel-Europe R&D Directorate for the EU Framework Program (ISERD), "Israel Participation in FP7—Update 23 July 2009," *ISERD* 2009, <http://www.iserd .org.il/images/public/About/FP7/statistics/230709_iserd_stat.pdf> (17 August 2009).

4. See Nellie Munin, "Israeli-European Cooperation under the Galileo Programme: The Sky is (Not) the Limit," in *The Monitor of the Israeli-European Policy Network*, ed. Roby Nathanson and Stephan Stetter (Tel-Aviv and Vienna: Friedrich-Ebert-Stiftung, 2006), 54–71.

5. Konrad-Adenauer-Stiftung and Sharon Pardo, *Measuring the Attitudes of Israelis toward the European Union and its Member States* (Jerusalem: Konrad-Adenauer-Stiftung, 2007); Konrad-Adenauer-Stiftung and Sharon Pardo, *Measuring the Attitudes of Israelis toward the European Union and its Member States* (Jerusalem: Konrad-Adenauer-Stiftung, 2009). See also table 4.3 in chapter 4.

6. See Claire Spencer, "New Challenges for EU-Israel Relations After the Gaza War," *Israeli European Policy Network* April 2009, <http://www.fes.org.il/src/Spencer (1).pdf> (29 July 2009).

7. Tzipi Livni as foreign minister spoke about Israel's efforts to upgrade relations with NATO as part of its broader foreign policy to bolster Israel's multilateral diplomacy; Tzipi Livni, "Address by Foreign Minister Tzipi Livni at the NATO-Israel Conference," *NATO* 22 October 2007, <http://www.nato.int/med dial/2007/071022-nato-israel.pdf> (10 July 2009). See also Uzi Arad, Oded Eran and Tommy Steiner, "Anchoring Israel to the Euro-Atlantic Community: Further Upgrading and Institutionalizing NATO-Israel Relations," *The Seventh Annual Herzliya Conference* 2007, <http://www.herzliyaconference.org/Eng/_Articles/Article .asp?CategoryID=225&ArticleID=1601> (10 July 2009).

8. See Gerald M. Steinberg, "Examining European Funding Radical NGOs," *NGO Monitor* 2006, < http://www.ngo-monitor.org/data/images/File/examining_eu ropean_funding_for_radical_ngos.pdf> (12 July 2009).

9. <http://www.mfa.gov.il> (29 July 2009).

10. See Clara Marina O'Donnell, "The EU, Israel and Hamas," *Centre for European Reform Working Paper* 2008, <http://www.cer.org.uk/pdf/wp_820.pdf> (29 July 2009); Clara Marina O'Donnell, "The EU's Approach to Israel and the Palestinians: A Move in the Right Direction," *Centre for European Reform Policy Brief* 2009, <http://www.cer.org.uk/pdf/pb_israel_18june09.pdf> (29 July 2009).

11. Council of the European Union, "Press Release. 2951st Meeting General Affairs and External Relations. Luxembourg 15 and 16 June 2009," *Council of the*

European Union 2009, <http://www.consilium.europa.eu/uedocs/cms_Data/docs/pressdata/en/gena/108525.pdf> (22 July 2009).

12. Javier Solana, "Ditchley Foundation Annual Lecture by Javier Solana, EU High Representative for CFSP 'Europe's Global Role—What Next Steps?'" *Council of the European Union* 11 July 2009, <http://www.consilium.europa.eu/uedocs/cms_data/docs/pressdata/EN/discours/109193.pdf> (27 July 2009).

13. Solana also envisioned that the UN would accept the Palestinian state as a full member, and set a timetable for implementing the peace accord; Javier Solana, "Ditchley Foundation Annual Lecture."

14. A debate over talking with Hamas is also emerging in American circles. In the summer of 2009, former U.S. president Jimmy Carter met with Hamas leaders in Damascus and Gaza. See also Paul Scham and Osama Abu-Irshaid, "Hamas: Ideological Rigidity, Political Flexibility," *United States Institute for Peace Special Report* 224, June 2009, <http://www.usip.org/files/resources/Special%20Report%20224_Hamas.pdf> (12 July 2009).

15. General Secretariat of the Council, "Eighth Meeting of the EU-Israel Association Council: Statement of the European Union 16 June 2008," *General Secretariat of the Council* 2008, <http://www.delisr.ec.europa.eu/english/whatsnew.asp?id=1003> (22 July 2009).

16. At the same time, EU leaders also agreed, at the request of Israel, to shelve the publication of a new EU Action Strategy Paper for Peace in the Middle East; See European Commission, "The EU Action Strategy for Peace in the Middle East: The Way Forward," *European Commission*, (November 2008).

Selected Bibliography

Ahiram, Ephraim, and Alfred Tovias., eds. *Whither EU-Israeli Relations? Common and Divergent Interests*. Frankfurt am Main: Peter Lang, 1995.

Aliboni, Roberto. "Diplomatic Opportunities After Israeli-Hezbollah Conflict." *The International Spectator* 41, no.4 (2006): 101–7.

Aliboni, Roberto, Ahmed Driss, Tobias Schumacher, and Alfred Tovias. "Putting the Mediterranean Union in Perspective." *EuroMeSCo Paper* 68. 2008.

Allen, David. "The Euro-Arab Dialogue." *Journal of Common Market Studies* 16, no. 4 (1978): 323–42.

Allen, David, and Alfred Pijpers., eds. *European Foreign Policy Making and the Arab-Israeli Conflict*. London: Pinter, 1984.

Asseburg, Muriel. "The EU and the Middle East Conflict: Tackling the Main Obstacle to Euro-Mediterranean Partnership." *Mediterranean Politics* 8, no. 2–3 (2003): 174–95.

Asseburg, Muriel, and Volker Perthes. "After Gaza: What the United States and Europe Must Do in the Middle East." *Internationale Politik Global Edition* 10, no. 1 (2009): 42–45.

Avineri, Shlomo, and Werner Weidenfeld., eds. *Integration and Identity Challenges to Europe and Israel*. Bonn: Europa Union Verlag, 1999.

Bechev, Dimitar, and Kalypso Nicolaidis. "The Union for the Mediterranean: A Genuine Breakthrough or More of the Same?" *The International Spectator* 43, no. 3 (2008): 13–20.

Behrendt, Sven, and Christian-Peter Hanelt., eds. *Bound to Cooperate—Europe and the Middle East*. Gütersloh: Bertelsmann Foundation Publishers, 2000.

Blanchet, Thérèse, Risto Piipponen, and Maria Westman-Clément. *The Agreement on the European Economic Area (EEA): A Guide to the Free Movement of Goods and Competition Rules.* Oxford: Clarendon Press, 1994.

Boehnke, Klaus., ed. *Israel and Europe: A Complex Relationship.* Wiesbaden: Deutscher Universitäts-Verlag, 2003.

Brown, Nathan J. "Principled or Stubborn? Western Policy toward Hamas." *The International Spectator* 43, no.4 (2008): 73–87.

Cameron, Fraser., ed. *Bridges Over the Mediterranean? European and US Perspectives.* Jerusalem: The Helmut Kohl Institute for European Studies, 2004.

Chopra, Jarat. "Third Party Monitoring in the Israeli-Palestinian Conflict." *The International Spectator* 38, no.4 (2003): 33–45.

Dachs, Gisela, and Joel Peters. "Israel and the EU, the Troubled Relationship: Between Perceptions and Reality." Pp. 317–33 in *Reader of the Israeli-European Policy Network,* edited by Roby Nathanson and Stephan Stetter. Tel-Aviv and Vienna: Friedrich-Ebert-Stiftung, 2005.

Del Sarto, Raffaella A. *Contested State Identities and Regional Security in the Euro-Mediterranean Area.* Houndmills: Palgrave Macmillan, 2006.

———. "Region-Building, European Union Normative Power and Contested Identities: The Case of Israel." Pp. 296–333 in *The Convergence of Civilizations: Constructing a Mediterranean Region,* edited by Emanuel Adler, Federica Bicchi, Beverly Crawford and Raffaella A. Del Sarto. Toronto: University of Toronto Press, 2006.

———. "Wording and Meaning(s): EU-Israeli Political Cooperation according to the ENP Action Plan." *Mediterranean Politics* 11, no. 1 (2007): 59–74.

Del Sarto, Raffaella A., and Tobias Schumacher, "From EMP to ENP: What's at Stake with the European Neighbourhood Policy towards the Southern Mediterranean?" *European Foreign Affairs Review* 10, no. 1 (2005): 17–38.

Del Sarto, Raffaella A., and Alfred Tovias. "Caught Between Europe and the Orient: Israel and the EMP." *The International Spectator* 36, no. 4 (2001): 91–105.

Don Harpaz, Marcia. "Israel's Trade Relations with the European Union: The Case for Diversification." *Mediterranean Politics* 13, no. 3 (2008): 391–417.

Dosenrode, Søren, and Anders Stubkjær. *The European Union and the Middle East.* London: Sheffield Academic Press, 2002.

Douma, Wybe Th. "Israel and the Palestinian Authority." Pp. 433–61 in *The European Union and Its Neighbours: A Legal Appraisal of the EU's Policies of Stabilisation, Partnership and Integration,* edited by Steven Blockmans and Adam Lazowski. The Hague: T.M.C Asser Press, 2006.

Dror, Yehezkel, and Sharon Pardo. "Approaches and Principles for an Israeli Grand Strategy towards the European Union." *European Foreign Affairs Review* 11, no. 1 (2006): 17–44.

Duchêne, Francois. "Israel in the Eyes of the Europeans: A Speculative Essay." Pp. 11–32 in *Europe and Israel: Troubled Neighbours,* edited by Ilan Greilsammer and Joseph H. H. Weiler. New York: Walter de Gruyter, 1980.

Einhorn, Talia. *The Role of the Free Trade Agreement between Israel and the EEC.* Baden-Baden: Nomos, 1994.

Emerson, Michael, and Nathalie Tocci. *The Rubik Cube of the Wider Middle East.* Brussels: Centre for European Policy Studies, 2003.

Eran, Oded. "The Impact of Operation Cast Lead on Israel-EU Relations." *Israeli-European Policy Network.* 2009. <http://www.fes.org.il/src/PaperOdedEran(5).pdf> (29 July 2009).

European Communities. "Euro-Mediterranean Agreement Establishing an Association between the European Communities and their Member States, of the One Part, and the State of Israel, of the Other Part." *Official Journal of the European Communities* 2000/L 147/3, (21 November 2000).

European Union–Israel Association Council. "EU/Israel Action Plan." *European Union–Israel Association Council.* 2004. <http://ec.europa.eu/world/enp/pdf/action_plans/israel_enp_ap_final_en.pdf> (20 July 2009).

Gershowitz, Suzanne, and Emanuele Ottolenghi. "Europe's Problem with Ariel Sharon." *Middle East Quarterly.* 2005. <http://www.meforum.org/743/europes-problem-with-ariel-sharon> (29 July 2009).

Gerstenfeld, Manfred. *Israel and Europe: An Expanding Abyss?* Jerusalem: Jerusalem Center for Public Affairs and the Adenauer Foundation, 2005.

———. *European-Israeli Relations: Between Confusion and Change?* Jerusalem: Jerusalem Center for Public Affairs and the Adenauer Foundation, 2006.

Giersch, Herbert., ed. *The Economic Integration of Israel in the EEC.* Tübingen: Mohr, 1980.

Greilsammer, Ilan, and Joseph H. H. Weiler., eds. *Europe and Israel: Troubled Neighbours.* New York: Walter de Gruyter, 1980.

Grgic, Borut. "The New Security Front: How to Make Europe Count in the Middle East." *Internationale Politik Global Edition* 7, no. 4 (2006): 72–76.

Hanelt, Christian-Peter, and Almut Möller., eds. *Bound to Cooperate II—Europe and the Middle East.* Gütersloh: Verlag Bertelsmann Stiftung, 2008.

Harpaz, Guy. "Enhanced Relations Between the European Union and the State of Israel under the European Neighbourhood Policy: Some Legal and Economic Implications." *Legal Issues of Economic Integration* 31, no. 4 (2004): 257–75.

———. "The Dispute over the Treatment of Products Exported to the European Union from the Golan Heights, East Jerusalem, the West Bank and the Gaza Strip—The Limits of Power and the Limits of the Law." *Journal of World Trade* 38, no. 6 (2004): 1049–58.

———. "A Proposed Model for Enhanced EU-Israeli Relations: Prevailing Legal Arrangements and Prospective Juridical Challenges." *Journal of World Trade* 40, no. 6 (2006): 1115–44.

———. "Normative Power Europe and the Problem of a Legitimacy Deficit: An Israeli Perspective." *European Foreign Affairs Review* 12, no. 1 (2007): 89–109.

———. "Mind the Gap: Narrowing the Legitimacy Gap in EU-Israeli Relations." *European Foreign Affairs Review* 13, no. 1 (2008): 117–37.

Heller, Mark A. *Europe and the Middle East: New Tracks to Peace?* Tel Aviv: Friedrich-Ebert-Stiftung, 1999.

Herman, Lior. "An Action Plan or a Plan for Action? Israel and the European Neighbourhood Policy." *Mediterranean Politics* 11, no. 3 (2006): 371–94.

Hershco, Tsilla. "French Middle East Policy in the Sarkozy Era: Continuity or Disruption?" *The Israel Journal of Foreign Affairs* 1, no. 3 (2008): 23–33.

Hershco, Tsilla, and Amos Schupak. "France, the EU Presidency and Implications for the Middle East Conflict." *The Israel Journal of Foreign Affairs* 3, no. 2 (2009): 63–73.

Hillman, Arye L., and Zvi Sussman., eds. *Europe 1992: The Perspective from Israel.* Tel Aviv: Israeli Institute for Applied Economic Policy Review, 1991.

Hirsch, Moshe. "The 1995 Trade Agreement Between the European Communities and Israel: Three Unresolved Issues." *European Foreign Affairs Review* 1, no. 1(1996): 87–123.

———. "Rules of Origin as Trade or Foreign Policy Instruments? The European Union Policy on Products Manufactured in the Settlements in the West Bank and the Gaza Strip." *Fordham International Law Journal* 26, (2003): 572–94.

Hirsch, Moshe, Eyal Inbar, and Tal Sadeh. *The Future Relations Between Israel and the European Communities—Some Alternatives.* Tel Aviv: Bursi, 1996.

Hollis, Rosemary. "The Politics of Israeli-European Economic Relations." Pp. 118–34 in *Peace in the Middle East: The Challenge for Israel,* edited by Efraim Karsh. London: Frank Cass, 1994.

———. "Europe and the Middle East: Power by Stealth?" *International Affairs* 73, no. 1 (1997): 15–29.

Ifestos, Panayiotis. *European Political Cooperation: Towards a Framework of Supranational Diplomacy?* Aldershot: Avebury, 1987.

Jawad, Haiifaa A. *Euro-Arab Relations: A Study in Collective Diplomacy.* Reading: Ithaca Press, 1992.

Laufer, Leopold Yehuda. "The European Union and Israel: A Political and Institutional Appraisal." *Davis Papers on Israel's Foreign Policy.* 1997.

Lerman, Eran. *The Mediterranean Idea: Envisioning a Brighter Future for All the Peoples of the Mediterranean.* Jerusalem: American Jewish Committee, 2007.

Malanczuk, Peter. "The Legal Framework of the Economic Relations Between Israel and the European Union." Pp. 263–79 in *Israel Among the Nations,* edited by Alfred E. Kellermann, Kurt Siehr and Talia Einhorn. Leiden: Brill Academic Publishers, 1999.

Maresceau, Marc, and Erwan Lannon., eds. *The EU's Enlargement and Mediterranean Strategies: A Comparative Analysis.* Houndmills: Palgrave, 2001.

Munin, Nellie. *The EU and Israel: State of the Play* (Hebrew). Jerusalem: Israel Ministry of Finance, 2003.

Münster, Katharina von. "With a Stroke of a Pen: Israel's Image in the European Media." Pp. 282–305 in *The Monitor of the Israeli-European Policy Network,* edited by Roby Nathanson and Stephan Stetter. Tel-Aviv and Vienna: Friedrich-Ebert-Stiftung, 2006.

Nathanson, Roby, and Stephan Stetter., eds. *Reader of the Israeli-European Policy Network*. Tel-Aviv: Friedrich-Ebert-Stiftung, 2005.

———, eds. *The Monitor of the Israeli-European Policy Network*. Tel-Aviv and Vienna: Friedrich-Ebert-Stiftung, 2006.

———, eds. *The Middle East Under Fire? EU-Israel Relations in a Region Between War and Conflict Resolution*. Tel-Aviv and Berlin: Friedrich-Ebert-Stiftung, 2007.

———, eds. *Renewing the Middle East: Climate Changes in Security and Energy and the New Challenges for EU-Israel Relations*. Tel-Aviv and Brussels: Friedrich-Ebert-Stiftung, 2008.

O'Donnell, Clara Marina. "The EU, Israel and Hamas." *Centre for European Reform Working Paper*. 2008. <http://www.cer.org.uk/pdf/wp_820.pdf> (3 August 2009).

———. "The EU's Approach to Israel and the Palestinians: A Move in the Right Direction." *Centre for European Reform Policy Brief*. 2009. <http://www.cer.org.uk/pdf/pb_israel_18june09.pdf> (3 August 2009).

Ohana, David. "Israel Towards a Mediterranean Identity." Pp. 84–99 in *Integration and Identity Challenges to Europe and Israel*, edited by Shlomo Avineri and Werner Wedienfeld. Bonn: Europa Union Verlag, 1999.

———. "Mediterraneans or Crusaders? Israel Geopolitical Images Between East and West." *International Journal of Euro-Mediterranean Studies* 1, no. 1 (2008): 7–32.

Pardo, Sharon. "The New Political-Organisation Challenge of the Jews of the Enlarged European Union." Pp. 262–71 in *Integrating with the European Union: Accession, Association and Neighbourhood Policy*, edited by Ladislav Cabada and Michal Mravinač. Plzeň: University of Public Administration and International Relations and Metropolitan University Prague, 2008.

———. "Toward an Ever Closer Partnership: A Model for a New Euro-Israeli Partnership." *EuroMeSCo Paper* 72. 2008.

———. "Between Attraction and Resistance: Israeli Views of the European Union." Pp. 70–86 in *External Perceptions of the European Union as a Global Actor*, edited by Sonia Lucarelli and Lorenzo Fioramonti. Oxon and New York: Routledge, 2009.

———. "Going West: Guidelines for Israel's Integration in the European Union." *The Israel Journal of Foreign Affairs* 3, no. 2 (2009): 51–62.

———. "Israel and the European Union: Public, Elite, Civil Society and Media Perceptions of the Union." Forthcoming in *Mediterranean Perspectives on International Relations*, edited by Stephen C. Calleya. Malta: Mediterranean Academy of Diplomatic Studies, 2009.

———. "Partnership without Membership: What the EU Can Offer Israel within the Framework of the European Neighbourhood Policy." Pp 119–40 in *The European Neighbourhood Policy and the Southern Mediterranean: Drawing from the Lessons of Enlargement*, edited by Michelle Comelli, Atila Eralp, and Cigdem Ustun. Rome and Ankara: Italian Institute for International Affairs and the Middle East Technical University, 2009.

Peters, Joel. *Pathways to Peace: The Multilateral Arab-Israeli Peace Talks.* London: Royal Institute of International Affairs, 1996.

———. "Europe, the Middle East Peace Process and the Barcelona Process: Competition or Convergence?" *The International Spectator* 33, no. 4 (1998): 63–76.

———. "Europe and the Middle East Peace Process." Pp. 295–316 in *The Foreign Policies of the European Union's Mediterranean States and Applicant Countries in the 1990s,* edited by Stelios Stavridis, Theodore Couloumbis, Thanos Veremis and Neville Waites. London: Macmillan, 1999.

———. "Europe and the Arab-Israeli Peace Process: The Declaration of the European Council of Berlin and Beyond." Pp. 150–71 in *Bound to Cooperate—Europe and the Middle East,* edited by Sven Behrendt and Christian-Peter Hanelt. Gütersloh: Bertelsmann Foundation Publishers, 2000.

———. "Practices and Their Failure: Arab-Israeli Relations and the Barcelona Process." Pp. 212–35 in *The Convergence of Civilizations: Constructing a Mediterranean Region,* edited by Emanuel Adler, Federica Bicchi, Beverly Crawford, and Raffaella A. Del Sarto. Toronto: University of Toronto Press, 2006.

Phinnemore, David. *Association: Stepping-Stone or Alternative to EU Membership.* Sheffield: Sheffield Academic Press, 1999.

Pomfret, Richard W. T., and Benjamin Toren. *Israel and the European Common Market: An Appraisal of the 1975 Free Trade Agreement.* Tübingen: Mohr, 1980.

Richmond, Oliver P. "Sharing Sovereignty and the Politics of Peace: Evaluating the EU's 'Catalytic' Framework in the Eastern Mediterranean." *International Affairs* 82, no. 1 (2006): 149–76.

Sachar, Howard M. *Israel and Europe: An Appraisal in History.* New York: Vintage Books, 1998.

Sadeh, Tal. "Israel and a Euro-Mediterranean Internal Market." *Mediterranean Politics* 9, no. 1 (2004): 29–52.

Sayigh, Yezid. "Changing Dynamics in Palestinian Politics." *The International Spectator* 41, no. 2 (2006): 69–86.

Shavit, Yaacov, and Jehuda Reinharz. *Glorious, Accursed Europe. An Essay on Jews, Israelis, Europe and Western Culture* (Hebrew). Tel Aviv: Am Oved, 2006.

Shlaim, Avi, and George N. Yannopoulos., eds. *The EEC and the Mediterranean Countries.* Cambridge: Cambridge University Press, 1976.

Shpiro, Shlomo. "EU-Israeli Security, Justice and Home Affairs Cooperation: One Year into the Action Plan." Pp. 135–85 in *The Monitor of the Israeli-European Policy Network,* edited by Roby Nathanson and Stephan Stetter. Tel-Aviv and Vienna: Friedrich-Ebert-Stiftung, 2006.

———. "Europe's Watch in the Middle East: European Peacekeepers Have a Mixed Record in the Region." *Internationale Politik Global Edition* 9, no. 1 (2008): 74–80.

Shpiro, Shlomo, and Klaus Becher. "European-Israeli Security and Defence Co-operation: Expectations and Impediments." Pp. 152–74 in *Reader of the Israeli-European Policy Network*, edited by Roby Nathanson and Stephan Stetter. Tel-Aviv and Vienna: Friedrich-Ebert-Stiftung, 2005.

Spencer, Claire. "New Challenges for EU-Israel Relations After the Gaza War." *Israeli-European Policy Network*. 2009. <http://www.fes.org.il/src/PaperClaireSpencer.pdf> (29 July 2009).

Steinberg, Gerald M. "Learning the Lessons of the European Union's Failed Middle East Policies." *Jerusalem Viewpoints* 510, (2004).

Stetter, Stephan. "Democratization without Democracy? The Assistance of the European Union for Democratization Processes in Palestine." *Mediterranean Politics* 8, no. 2–3 (2003): 153–73.

Tocci, Nathalie. "Conflict Resolution in the Neighbourhood: Comparing EU Involvement in Turkey's Kurdish Question and in the Israeli-Palestinian Conflict." *Mediterranean Politics* 10, no. 2 (2005): 125–46.

———. "The Widening Gap Between Rhetoric and Reality in EU Policy towards the Israeli-Palestinian Conflict." *CEPS Working Paper* 217. (2005).

———. "What Went Wrong? The Impact of Western Politics Towards Hamas and Hizbollah." *CEPS Policy Brief* 135. (2007).

Touval, Yonatan. "Combating Anti-Semitism: Monitoring the EU-Israel Action Plan." Pp. 246–59 in *The Monitor of the Israeli-European Policy Network*, edited by Roby Nathanson and Stephan Stetter. Tel-Aviv and Vienna: Friedrich-Ebert-Stiftung, 2006.

Tovias, Alfred. "Israel between Europe and America: The Status of Israel in a World of Rival Trading Blocks." *History of European Ideas* 18, no. 5 (1994): 697–710.

———. "Israel and the Barcelona Process." *EuroMeSCo Working Papers* 3. 1998.

———. "Israeli Policy Perspectives on the Euro-Mediterranean Partnership in the Context of EU Enlargement." *Mediterranean Politics* 8, no. 2–3 (2003): 214–32.

———. "Mapping Israel's Policy Options Regarding its Future Institutionalised Relations with the European Union." *CEPS Middle East & Euro-Med Working Paper* 3. 2003.

———. "Exploring the 'Pros' and 'Cons' of Switzerland's and Norway's Model of Relations with the EU: What Can be Learned From these Two Countries' Experience by Israel." *Cooperation and Conflict* 41, no. 2 (2006): 203–22.

———. "Spontaneous vs. Legal Approximation: The Europeanization of Israel." *European Journal of Law Reform* 9, no. 3 (2007): 485–500.

Tovias, Alfred, and Amichai A. Magen. "Reflections from the New Near Outside: An Israeli Perspective on the Institutional Impact of EU Enlargement." *European Foreign Affairs Review* 10, no. 5 (2005): 399–425.

Veit, Winfried. *A European Perspective for Israel: A Key to Solving the Middle East Conflict*. Herzliya: Friedrich-Ebert-Stiftung, 2003.

Youngs, Richard. *Europe and the Middle East in the Shadow of September 11*. Boulder: Lynne Rienner, 2006.

Zemer, Lior and Sharon Pardo. "The Qualified Zones in Transition: Navigating the Dynamics of the Euro-Israeli Customs Dispute." *European Foreign Affairs Review* 8, no. 1 (2003): 51–75.

———. "The European Neighbourhood Policy and Israel: Choosing the Judicial Forum in Light of the European Constitution." Pp. 116–34 in *The Monitor of the Israeli-European Policy Network*, edited by Roby Nathanson and Stephan Stetter. Tel-Aviv and Vienna: Friedrich-Ebert-Stiftung, 2006.

Index